HERO IN THE STORM

I welcome this return of Mark Fellows to the publishing world. More than a mere chronicler of ecclesial history, Fellows is a true story-teller, a master of literary style who writes with the passion of a Catholic soul. A glance at any page of this new work will show that it is an important contribution to understanding at the deepest level the situation in which we now find ourselves since the conquering march of the zeitgeist made its way into the Church at Vatican II.

— **CHRISTOPHER FERRARA**, author of *Liberty, the God That Failed*

There is no doubt in my mind that the path forward for Catholics in the post-conciliar era demands a thorough understanding of the pontificate and legacy of Pope Pius IX. One simply cannot grasp the significance of calling the documents of Vatican-II a "counter-Syllabus" without first understanding the impetus behind the Syllabus of Errors itself, nor can one make sense of the Revolution of today without first placing it within the broader context of the Revolution of the tumultuous 19th century. It is certain that the trajectory of the post-conciliar period of the Catholic Church will hinge on the legacy we make of Pope Pius IX and the documents, ideas, and actions of his pontificate. Mark Fellows in *Hero in the Storm* makes an excellent contribution to this effort, with vivid accounts of the Fall of Rome, the charged atmosphere behind the First Vatican Council and a comprehensive vision of the 19th-century Papal States, Fellows provides the reader with a sense of clarity, depth, and familiarity with the life and times of Pope Pius IX.

— **MURRAY W. RUNDUS**, Managing Editor, *Catholic Family News*

HERO
IN THE STORM

*Pius IX Against
the Revolution*

MARK FELLOWS

AROUCA
PRESS

Arouca Press, Waterloo N2J 0A5
© 2025 by Mark Fellows
www.aroucapress.com

ISBN: 978-1-998492-41-1 (pbk)
ISBN: 978-1-998492-42-8 (hc)

On the cover:
Pius IX (top) and below, from left to right:
Giuseppe Garibaldi, Victor Emmanuel II,
Giuseppe Mazzini

Dedicated, with love, to
Nelia Cuanico Fellows

CONTENTS

T HIS is the story of a man who ruled the Roman Catholic Church when an emerging modern society challenged the truths and beliefs he was sworn to protect and defend.

Although this happened over a century ago, the same fight for truth continues today. Is truth like shifting sand, revisable at will? Or are some truths always true whether we believe them or not? These questions remain critical because what we believe directly influences our behavior, our relationships, and our world.

Some decades ago, Yves Chiron wrote an excellent biography of Pius IX.[1] My biography, though different in tone and emphasis, is not meant to compete with his. Rather, it joins voices with his and many others around the world in revealing and celebrating the life of a remarkable man: Giovanni Maria Mastai-Feretti.

Blessed Pius IX was pope for thirty-two years. For over three decades his Church was repeatedly attacked. His territories were illegally seized by force; many of his citizens were killed and imprisoned; he himself was imprisoned; he was shot at; he was exiled from Rome; the rights of the Church were trampled upon; its property and buildings were confiscated; and finally, Rome itself was taken from the Church.

Through those long, dark years, *Pio Nono* (as he was known) never surrendered. He fought back emphatically with his words and actions and kept his remarkable sense of humor throughout. He is a superb example of a Christian response to a godless society.

This man is a hero. Here is his story.

---

[1] Yves Chiron, *Pius IX: The Man and the Myth*, trans. Graham Harrison (Kansas City, MO: Angelus Press, 2005).

CHAPTER 1

° °

THE LANDSCAPE

I T was 1881 and Italy's prime minister was a Freemason named Agostino Depretis.[1] Possessing "an instinctive prejudice" against the Church, this champion of the free press attempted to make it a crime for priests to publicly criticize his rule. Consequently, the Vatican thought it prudent to move the coffin at night.

The modest funeral procession left the Vatican Basilica quietly. Lanterns and candles lit the way for the dead pope's coffin. The procession had barely begun its journey toward the Basilica of San Lorenzo when it was accosted by "a well-known band of bad men" intent on heaving the coffin into the Tiber River. The reigning pope, Leo XIII, recalled with indignation that:

> As their numbers and audacity increased so they went on increasing in their efforts to create tumult and terror; they uttered the most atrocious blasphemies...The funeral cortege was hemmed in by crowds of angry men, whose looks and voices threatened them at every step, while again and again they attacked the procession with volleys of stones or with blows...They again and again hurled a shower of stones at the hearse, crying out repeatedly that the unburied body should be cast forth...This shameful scene lasted all through the long route, during the space of two hours.[2]

---

[1] Denis Mack Smith, *Italy: A Modern History*, rev. ed., (Ann Arbor: University of Michigan Press, 1969), 222. Smith, a non-Catholic secular historian, describes Depretis as a Freemason and his policies as reflecting "an instinctive prejudice against" the Church.

[2] Rev. Bernard O'Reilly, *The Life of Pope Leo XIII: From His Personal Memoirs*, (Philadelphia: John C. Winston Company, 1903), 440–442.

The "bad men" were Freemasons.[3] The coffin contained
the corpse of Leo's predecessor, Pope Pius IX. More than a
century later, reaction to the Catholic Church's beatification
of Pius IX proved Pio Nono (as he is commonly known)
remains well hated by the self-proclaimed friends of progress
and toleration.

Time magazine, *The Washington Post,* and *The New York
Times* were negative to the point of bitterness in their cover-
age of Pius' September 2000 beatification. "These are dismal
times for Catholicism," moaned the *London Financial Times,*
calling the beatification a "tragic mystery," and characterizing
Pius as "dripping with vanity." After vilifying John Paul II as
an arch-reactionary, the grimly hysterical article concluded
by calling for his resignation.[4]

INTOLERANCE BY THE TOLERANT?

European liberals and progressives took their cues from
a daylong seminar hosted by an Italian Jewish organization[5] that threatened to break off dialogue with postconciliar
peace brokers in the Vatican. Another Jewish publication,
the magazine *Shalom,* called Pius a "womanizer," a "gambler,"
"arrogant," "cruel," and a "sinister figure."[6]

Time magazine spoke of Pius IX's "ham-fisted treatment
of the Jews,"[7] a possible reference to Pius' involvement in the
controversial Mortara Affair. In 1858 a six-year-old Jewish
boy named Edgardo Mortara was taken from his family to
be raised Catholic after it was discovered that the boy, when
seriously ill as a baby, had been secretly baptized by the
Mortara family's Catholic servant.

Despite the international uproar over the event Pius IX

---

[3] *Inside The Vatican,* March 2000, 51.
[4] *London Financial Times,* September 8, 2000. The article, in all its
melodramatic, semi-coherent glory, is a fun read.
[5] Italy's Union of Jewish Communities, "Pius IX, the Church and the
Jews, Between Religion and Politics in the *Risorgimento* Era," Presen-
tation, Rome, June 2000.
[6] As quoted by *Inside The Vatican,* August–September 2000, 71.
[7] *Time,* September 4, 2000.

refused to order the return of young Edgardo to his family. Instead, he took a special interest in the boy, who grew up to become a priest and spent much of his adult life trying to convert Jews.

Mortara's great-great-niece, Elena, joined hundreds of other Jews who came to Rome to protest on the night before Pius' beatification. The next day John Paul II said this about Pius' elevation:

> By beatifying one of its sons the Church does not celebrate particular historical choices he made, but rather points him out for imitation and veneration for his virtues, and praising the divine grace that shines in them.[8]

These remarks, *The Jerusalem Post* reported, were "met with regret in Israel over its insensitivity to Jewish concerns." The *Post* went on to express a marked preference for the "righteous gentile," John XXIII (beatified with Pius IX in 2000) over the villainous Pio Nono who, according to the *Post*, was not merely "an extreme anti-Semite," but "a rigid traditionalist"[9] to boot.

Joining the chorus were Hans Küng, Edward Schillebeeckx, and seventeen other progressive theologians who, in the journal *Concilium*, denounced Pius IX for being against "reform" and, of course, for being hostile toward Jews. Not to be outdone, an international organization of misfits known as *We Are Church* proclaimed the beatification of Pius IX "disgraceful." [10]

So things haven't changed much since that dark night in Rome over a century ago: Pius' enemies are still trying to throw him in the river. Talk about sore winners. In addition to relentlessly persecuting the Church—not just in Europe but all over the world—the Revolution drove Pius IX from Rome, took the Papal States, and ultimately took Rome itself.

---

[8] *The Jerusalem Post*, September 4, 2000.
[9] *The Jerusalem Post*, September 5, 2000.
[10] *Inside The Vatican*, August–September 2000, 73.

The masterstroke was reserved for this century: an ecumenical council proclaimed as "the French Revolution in
the Church" by progressive Council Fathers and welcomed
as a "counter-*Syllabus*" by Cardinal (later pope) Ratzinger.
What more could be hoped for?

It seems Pius' enemies don't realize they have won. Or do
they sense, perhaps, that they really *haven't* won? For when
Pius' body was exhumed last year prior to his beatification,
it was found to be "almost perfectly preserved," his face
exuding a "striking serenity."[11] Plans are underway to place
the incorrupt body in a crystal casket for all to see.

Incorruption is one of many signs of predilection bestowed
upon Blessed Pope Pius IX. His patron was the Blessed Virgin Mary, and his papacy—the longest in history—was part
of the remarkable influence the Blessed Virgin exercised
during the nineteenth century, a watershed period in which
the decisive struggle between the serpent and *she who would
crush his head with her heel* entered a critical phase.

The human combatants were, on the one side, the anti-
Christian revolution which, via Freemasonry, continued to
tear Christian society from the Church that had created it—a
rending they called progress.

Opposing this was the Church, particularly Blessed Pius
IX, of whom his biographer, E. E. Y. Hales, concludes:

> It was Pio Nono's fate, after traveling with sym-
> pathy in his earlier years more than half way to
> meet the Revolution, to be compelled, though
> not naturally a fighter, to turn and withstand its
> pretensions. It was his glory that he confronted
> the tempest without flinching, and was faithful
> to the end.[12]

He fought, he persevered, and he remained faithful to
the end because he was a Marian pope. As Pius himself

[11] As reported in *Newsweek*, September 4, 2000.
[12] E. E. Y. Hales, *Pio Nono: Creator of the Modern Papacy* (New York:
P. J. Kenedy & Sons, 1954), 331.

put it, during one of the innumerable crises during his thirty-two-year pontificate: "I have the Blessed Virgin with me, I shall press on undeterred."[13] Surely her intercession helped Pius wrestle so mightily for decades against the Revolution.

It is hoped this examination of the life and times of Pius IX will illuminate this point. I will respond to some of the factually inaccurate, unhistorical criticisms and caricatures of Blessed Pius IX by placing his words and deeds squarely in their historical context—something rarely done in the English language. In the end readers will make up their own minds about it all.

---

[13] *La Contre-Réforme Catholique* (CRC), September 2000, online English edition, 1.

CHAPTER 2

. . . .

THE CHURCH &
THE REVOLUTION

E was born Giovanni Maria Mastai-Ferretti on
May 13, 1792, a few short months before the September Terror in Paris.[1] Giovanni was raised in
the Marches, a region of the Papal States bordering the Adri-
atic Sea. When he was six, the French Revolution arrived
in Italy and the Papal States, courtesy of General Napoleon
Bonaparte.

After the French army occupied Rome its officers tore
the Fisherman's Ring from the finger of Pope Pius VI. The
eighty-two-year-old pontiff was abducted and subjected to a
death march across the Alps. When Pius gave up the ghost
on August 29, 1799, the Revolution celebrated the death
of "the last Pope."[2]

Napoleon was ready to prevent a conclave in Rome but
could not prevent one in Venice; Pius VI had arranged
the change in location before his death. The Revolution's
revenge was to govern Rome and the Papal States according
to the Napoleonic Code, particularly in enforcing religious
liberty — for non-Catholics, anyway.

French influence during Napoleon's two invasions of Italy
caused the number of Masonic secret societies to multiply,
particularly in the Papal States. Hales notes:

> During the period of the French revolution, the
> Romagna had been incorporated...with the
> Marches (both were Papal States) in Napoleon's

---

[1] The September Terror occurred September 2–7, 1792, when the
revolutionary government, which installed itself without election in
1789, executed 1,200–1,400 Parisians.
[2] Henri Daniel-Rops, *The Church in an Age of Revolution, 1789–1870* (New
York: E. P. Dutton & Co., 1965), 54–58.

Kingdom of Italy. Thus had come about a break with old customs, and the indoctrination with the "principles of '89" and with the tenets of French Freemasonry, and then of Carbonarism (Italian Freemasonry).[3]

It was from these influences that Mastai-Ferretti's mother sought to shield her eleven-year-old son by sending him to the College of St. Michael in Volterra, a mountainous region of Tuscany. The school had been consecrated to the Blessed Virgin Mary by its founder, Father (later Saint) Joseph Calasanctius.

There young Mastai learned the "Crown of Twelve Stars," a devotion centered on the twelve privileges of Mary. The fourth privilege — "*Praised be God the Father who preserved the Virgin Mary from every stain at Her conception*"[4] — would shine brightly over the whole world a few short decades later.

Outside the Tuscan mountains, Napoleon was dueling with the next "last pope," Pius VII. The very fact there was a duel at all demonstrated the Revolution's failure to exterminate Catholicism in France or elsewhere. Napoleon, whose career began as an ally of the Jacobins during the French Revolution, was a baptized Catholic, a Freemason,[5] and an arch-realist who had no more love for the Church than he did for Masonry or the Revolution.

Each was a vehicle for his ambition. Bonaparte knew he could not undertake the conquering of Europe and the rest of the world without two things. First, he needed the blessing of international Masonry, and at the beginning of his career he had this. Second, he needed peace in France. This required a truce with the Church.

---

[3] Hales, *Pio Nono*, 23.
[4] Brother Francis of Mary of the Angels, *Blessed Pius IX, Pope and Doctor of the Immaculate*, CRC Online Edition, September 2000, 2.
[5] Mgr. George E. Dillon, D. D., *Grand Orient Freemasonry Unmasked* (1885; repr., Hawthorne, Calif.: Christian Book Club), chap. 10, "Napoleon and Freemasonry."

The concordat he signed with Pius VII was the price Napoleon paid to win French Catholic opinion. Freemasons hated Bonaparte for bargaining with Rome. Yet by the dawn of the nineteenth century, the Revolution was a spent force in France — glutted on murder, mayhem, and political and social anarchy. Napoleon imparted a desperately needed order to the First French Republic, which seemed incapable of building anything on the ruins it had created.

"THE VASSAL"

So when Napoleon appointed himself France's First Consul, and declared "I am the Revolution," the revolutionaries had to agree. They were cheered somewhat by Napoleon's vision: "The Pope will be my vassal."[6] Unfortunately for Bonaparte, Pius VII, despite signing the Concordat,[7] was neither weak nor a dupe.

He was, rather, a subtle, supple opponent who bent and bent but never broke. Events came to a head when Napoleon decided to become King of Italy and incorporate the Papal States into his new kingdom. This was how Bonaparte, in 1809, became the first emperor excommunicated by his "vassal."

Napoleon responded by branding Pius "a raving lunatic who must be locked up."[8] Once again, French soldiers kidnapped a pope, putting Pius in Savona for three years, then taking him to Fontainebleau, a transfer so difficult Pius received *Viaticum*[9] en route. The other tortures he suffered

---

[6] Daniel-Rops, *The Church in an Age of Revolution*, 93.

[7] The Concordat allowed the exiled French bishops — exiled because they were faithful to Rome — to be deposed by Napoleon, who then appointed his own bishops. All clergy were required to pledge allegiance to the secular state of France. In truth, the Concordat was a laundry list of Church concessions to the atheistic French government, and caused royalist and traditionalist Catholics to view Pius VII as a traitor to their cause.

[8] Albert Bessières, S. J., *Wife, Mother and Mystic (Blessed Anna-Maria Taigi)*, trans. Rev. Stephen Rigby (Westminster, Md.: The Newman Press, 1952), 158.

[9] The Latin word *viaticum* refers to the final Holy Communion of one's life. *Viaticum* means "along the road." It is food (Holy Communion)

during his five-year captivity remained largely unknown, except among Roman cardinals and prelates, who were informed of Pius' misfortunes in great detail by a humble, illiterate Roman housewife named Anna Maria Taigi.

Anna, the wife of a servant and mother of seven, had for years been receiving visions from a lighted orb that resembled the sun but contained people and future events portrayed in such detail as to astonish her spiritual director.

Pius VII corresponded with Anna, asking for her prayers and blessing her. He would have met with her publicly but feared increasing gossip. For much of her adult life Anna Maria's credibility—even her sanity—was attacked. It was a cross she bore with patience and mildness. As for her visions, her biographer notes:

> Anna Maria followed the tribulations of Pius VII hour by hour without intermission in her mysterious sun. By her means the cardinals, the prelates in residence in Rome, and the faithful generally, learnt of the sufferings of the prisoner...
>
> The Marquis Bandini, among other witnesses, testifies that about a year before the return of Pius VII, she told him the Pope would come back to his See with glory: 'She told me the exact date, saying that he would pontificate in St. Peter's on Whitsunday. All fell out precisely as she foretold. Thus on 24th May 1814 Anna assisted at the entry of the Holy Father into Rome.[10]

When Napoleon made Pius VII his prisoner he was the mightiest man in the world. Less than five years after being excommunicated, Bonaparte abdicated his power in the same palace at Fontainebleau where he had imprisoned the pope. Then he stole away, disguised as an Austrian soldier to escape the wrath of his French subjects. He died in exile on Elba.

---

for the final journey, given when one is about to die.
[10] Bessières, *Wife, Mother and Mystic*, 159.

Pius, on the other hand, began a slow, triumphal return to Rome. In Sinigaglia he met his distant cousin, Giovanni Mastai-Ferretti, who had returned home from his studies for the priesthood in Rome.[11] When Pius left Sinigaglia the twenty-two-year-old Mastai-Ferretti was with him. They entered Rome together. Pius VII would become Mastai's patron.

---

[11] Either because of his epilepsy or because of the political turmoil in the Eternal City.

° °

CHAPTER 3

A FREEMASON?

MASTAI'S studies for the priesthood continued to be interrupted by bouts of epilepsy that came without warning. In 1815 he was found unconscious on a street in Rome, the victim of another seizure. Mastai made a pilgrimage to the Holy House of Loreto, "to pour out his soul before the Heart of her who would always be his strength. From that pilgrimage dates the effective and definitive cure of his terrible malady."[1]

His cure appears to have been instant and permanent. Mastai petitioned Pius VII for a dispensation from the requirement of having another priest assist him at Mass as a precaution for seizures. After hearing him out, Pius replied: "We grant what you ask, dear son, because it is our conviction that this disease will never again afflict you."[2] He was right.

THE *CARBONARI*

Mastai became a priest on Holy Saturday, 1819. He celebrated his first Mass the next day, Easter Sunday, at St. Ann's Church, a chapel on the grounds of an orphanage for abandoned boys Mastai had served. His proud parents were also present.

In 1823 Pius VII sent Mastai on a diplomatic mission to Chile. By the time Mastai returned in 1825, Pius had died. His successor, Pope Leo XII, appointed Monsignor Mastai to direct St. Michael's, a large complex containing a reformatory, industrial school, and hospital.

---

[1] Pierre Fernessole, *Pie IX*, vol. 1 (Paris: Lethielleux, 1960), 26, as quoted in *CRC*, September 2000, online edition.
[2] Rev. Bernard O'Reilly, *A Life of Pius IX* (New York: P. F. Collier, 1877), 31–32.

Monsignor Mastai's administrative skills, spontaneous eloquence, and charity transformed St. Michael's into an impressive institution. His love of beauty sparked an art school at St. Michael's that, in a short time, became a conservatory of classical Roman art.

Mastai's skills were rewarded in 1827 when Pope Leo appointed him Archbishop of Spoleto, a troubled diocese in the Papal State of Umbria.

Temporal power over the Papal States had been restored to the Church at the Congress of Vienna. Austrian troops were stationed in northern Italy to enforce the change. The architect of the Vienna Restoration, Austria's Prince Klemens von Metternich, urged the reconstituted European monarchies to "suppress secret societies, that gangrene of society."[3] Metternich knew the enemy, and did what he could to prevent Masonry from attacking papal authority in the States.

He was battling the secret societies — determined, violent enemies who used secrecy as a weapon. This is now commonly admitted. Even a secular authority on 19th-century Italy like Denis Mack Smith is obliged to note: "Very soon after the Restoration of 1814–15, secret societies became active with the avowed policy of overthrowing the Vienna settlement."[4]

The societies were nowhere more active than in the Papal States, including Archbishop Mastai's diocese of Spoleto. The chief agitators were the *Carbonari*, an Italian version of the French Freemasonry imported by Napoleon, known as *Charbonnerie*. According to the secular historian Hales:

> This secret society of the "charcoal burners" had an interesting ideology, partly derived from French Freemasonry, partly from more obscure Italian sources. Their motto was "despotism

---

[3] . Prince Metternich, *Memoirs of Prince Metternich, 1815–1829*, ed. Prince Richard Metternich, vol. 3 (New York: Howard Fertig, 1970; repr. of Scribner and Sons, 1881), as presented electronically by Paul Halsall in the *Internet Modern History Sourcebook*.
[4] Smith, *Italy: A Modern History*, 11.

annihilated"—an achievement symbolized on a medal by the Goddess of Liberty slaying the Dragon of Tyranny.

The authority most particularly sought out for slaying was that of the Church, though this was not disclosed, explicitly, to any but those few who attained to the Seventh Grade of initiation.[5]

It was the Carbonari who organized the revolt of 1830–31. The violence in the Papal States spilled over into Rome itself and the new pope, Gregory XVI, was forced to ask Austrian troops to stop the violence. The Austrians proved an effective remedy. They chased the Carbonari from state to state, beating them at every turn.

The fleeing Carbonari army came to the walls of Spoleto. They threatened to take the town by violence if Archbishop Mastai did not open the gates. The Austrians likewise threatened Archbishop Mastai with occupation if he aided the Carbonari. It was a tough spot for the new archbishop. What would he do?

Mastai entered the Carbonari camp under a flag of truce. After distributing money and food he promised the Carbonari safe conduct home if they disbanded their army and stockpiled their weapons. Pinned between Austrian guns and a Catholic prelate, the revolutionaries pocketed the money and melted into the night.

Further bloodshed had been averted. Spoleto had been saved from the Carbonari and the Austrian army. Sighs of relief wafted through the darkness. From the Austrian camp came the gnashing of teeth.

Later, Archbishop Mastai was visited by another Carbonari, the prominent revolutionary Prince Louis Napoleon (nephew of Napoleon Bonaparte). With his mother in tow, the prince begged for refuge. Mastai allowed them to stay in his palace, arranged for young Louis' safe conduct through the Papal States, and sent the prince away with a sum of

money. Years later, Archbishop Mastai-Ferretti and Prince
Louis Napoleon would meet again under different titles, and
the contrast between Christian charity and revolutionary
honor would be stark indeed.

WAS MASTAI A MASON?

For now, the Austrians were heartily disgusted with Spoleto's archbishop. Their army had cornered the Carbonari and
Mastai helped the enemy escape. The Austrians had dearly
wished to apprehend Prince Louis, but Mastai spirited him
away as well. When the archbishop refused to assist Austrian
detectives in identifying revolutionaries living in Spoleto,
Austrian officials complained to Rome. In due course, Archbishop Mastai was summoned for a private audience with
Gregory XVI.

Gregory was a former Camaldolese monk and a former
liberal of sorts, at least in principle. Then he was forced
to flee Rome when Napoleon suppressed his order in 1807.
Experiencing firsthand the gap between revolutionary plati-
tudes and revolutionary behavior, Gregory became an intran-
sigent foe of anything that smelled like revolution.

Consequently, Pope Gregory was as angry with Mastai
as the Austrians. He delivered a blistering, highly negative
critique of his young archbishop's performance and ended
the audience without allowing Mastai a response.

Upon the archbishop's return, earthquakes rattled Spoleto
and much of Umbria. Mastai's resourcefulness and untiring
discharge of his pastoral duties during this crisis eased the
afflictions of all he came in contact with.

Having even fewer funds available than usual, he gave
a homeless woman an expensive silver branch candlestick
and told her to pawn it. The archbishop planned to hold
the ticket until he could afford to buy the piece back. The
woman was arrested at the pawn shop. When suspicious
authorities brought her before the archbishop a red-faced
Mastai admitted his role in the transaction.

Pope Gregory probably never heard that anecdote, but he was impressed enough by Archbishop Mastai's handling of the earthquake emergency to reconsider his critique. In 1833 the Pope appointed him to the vacant episcopacy in Imola.

The Spoletans sent a delegation to Pope Gregory, asking him to allow Mastai to remain in Spoleto. Their plea was a blend of sincerity and self-interest. The archbishop was respected, even loved, in his diocese. It was also true many Carbonari had returned to Spoleto, and they feared Gregory would appoint a bishop less tolerant of them than Mastai. But the Spoletans may as well have stayed at home, for Pope Gregory had made up his mind.

One may conclude from this that Mastai was a "fellow traveler." It is occasionally asserted that before becoming Pius IX, Mastai was a Freemason, or at least sympathetic to Masonry. The anecdotes above would support either assertion. It is, of course, very difficult to prove membership in a secret society. One allegation, that Mastai was enrolled in a lodge in Philadelphia, Pennsylvania, is simply ridiculous. Upon becoming Pius IX, he frequently and emphatically denounced Freemasonry.

Had he been involved in Masonry when younger, he would surely have publicly disavowed this association. Moreover, his formation, his purity, his piety, his zeal, and his devotion to the Blessed Virgin makes an allegiance to Masonry stand awkwardly alone. It is likely Mastai's intervention with the Carbonari in Spoleto arose from his wish to prevent bloodshed in his diocese. His coldness to Austrian investigators probably arose from his Italian nationalism, rather than fidelity to a secret society.

Mastai was as patriotic as any Italian, and most Italians of his time never dreamed of separating Church and State. The extent of Mastai's radical politics was his interest in the question of Italian unification, which at the time was closely allied with ending foreign involvement in Italian affairs. This was the wish of virtually every other Italian of the time, which is why Masonry used it as a selling point. To allege Mastai agreed with any other Masonic goals overstates things considerably.

The charge of liberalism seems more plausible, on the surface at least. Mastai's parents had a vague reputation for being enlightened, which was not a compliment. Pope Gregory's secretary of state, Lambruschini, complained: "Everyone in the Mastai family is a liberal, even the cats!"[6]

No specifics were provided for this statement. Mastai was never accused of being a follower of, say, Father Lamennais, who was condemned in 1832 by Gregory XVI[7] shortly after the Mastai's incident with the Carbonari in Spoleto.

Félicité Lamennais was a French priest who declared: "Let us not tremble before liberalism, let us Catholicize it."[8] Instead it was Lamennais who was catechized by the Revolution. He came to believe the will of the people was superior to everything, including divine revelation. His sincere attempts to convert the Revolution transformed him into a radical. Pope Gregory saw Lamennais had lost his faith, and publicly stated the truth. Lamennais left the priesthood and died in bitterness.

Regarding Mastai, however, Gregory seemed sufficiently satisfied with his orthodoxy to transfer him in 1833 to the see of Imola, a location which invariably produced cardinals. It is also reasonable to assume that the nine years Mastai had to wait for the cardinal's hat was Gregory's way of making sure he had the right man for the job.

The most accurate explanation of Mastai's liberalism comes from historian Henri Daniel-Rops:

---

[6] *CRC*, September 2000, online edition.
[7] Gregory XVI, *Mirari Vos*, August 15, 1832. In this encyclical, Gregory apologizes to the episcopate for not addressing them sooner and states that "From the first instant of Our pontificate" he was "carried away" into "the midst of a tempest," referring to the Carbonari uprisings in the Papal States. See *Mirari Vos* (Angelus Press edition, 1998), 1.
[8] Thomas Bokenkotter, *A Concise History of the Catholic Church* (New York: Image Books Doubleday, 1990) 266.

His so-called liberalism was nothing more than a true liberality of soul and the clear conviction that the methods employed hitherto against the new ideas were wrong. He judged it absurd to oppose railways, gaslight, suspension bridges, and scientific congresses — all novelties that could do the Church no harm.

He considered that the papal administration needed a thorough overhaul. Lastly, he believed that the best way for a ruler to halt the advance of revolution was not to have recourse to high-handed measures, but to set himself to win men's hearts by gentleness, generosity, and confidence.[9]

---

[9] Daniel-Rops, *The Church in an Age of Revolution*, 239.

CHAPTER 4

TO THE PAPACY

T HERE were few in Imola who mistook Bishop Mastai for a religious liberal, much less a Freemason. He was well liked, even loved, by many. A remarkable fact about Pius IX is that everyone—friend and foe—remarked on his striking personal appearance and personality. "He lived with us as though he were one of us," goes one account, "understanding our weaknesses...and managing to make us love his gentle gravity and respect his lovable kindness. Simply the thought of him made us behave well."[1]

An associate recalled that Mastai's face

> with its expression of goodness, intelligence and dispassionateness, makes a pleasant impression; his features, which it would be an understatement to describe as kindly, have nothing common or trivial about them, the overall effect being one of great dignity. The natural shape of the mouth is enhanced by a detail which only a very careful observer will notice: his habit of living for others and the sustained attention he pays to the various personalities and ideas that come before him have given his upper lip a nervous oscillation which lends an inexpressible grace to his smile.[2]

MAZZINI

There is no record of Giuseppe Mazzini being one of the "personalities" that came to Bishop Mastai's attention in Imola. Yet Mazzini was there, "plotting revolution" with his new organization *Young Italy*,[3] a secret society that owed

---

[1] *CRC*, September 2000, online edition.
[2] Ibid.
[3] Hales, *Pio Nono*, 37.

much to the Carbonari, of which Mazzini had been a member during the revolts of 1831.[4]

If Mazzini owed an organizational debt to the Carbonari, he owed a similar debt of ideas to apostate priest Félicité de Lamennais. The two were comrades for several years until Mazzini became disillusioned when, in his view, Father Lamennais did not apostatize far enough.

Mazzini is often portrayed as the darkest of the dark geniuses arrayed against the Church in the nineteenth century. He is accused of assassinating Nubius, the leader of the *Alta Vendita*, the highest Carbonari lodge in Italy. Then, "having wrenched the scepter of the dark Empire from that body, [Mazzini] continued with consummate ability to direct the revolutions of Europe."[5]

Mazzini emphatically denied being an assassin. Yet the bylaws of his own *Young Italy* explicitly ordered assassination, execution, and implacable vengeance against enemies in a matter-of-fact manner.[6] It was all a sharp contrast to Mazzini's flowing rhetoric about his "Faith In Humanity." In this religion, which Mazzini declared would replace Christianity, "Humanity is the only Messiah."[7]

This was not the faith of his childhood. Mazzini was raised a Catholic by his Jansenist mother. As an adult he claimed to believe in a transcendent God and heaven. Yet in his politic she was closer to his former comrade Father Lamennais; both seem to have mistaken man for God.

If Mastai never made Mazzini's acquaintance while in Imola, he would know him well enough later.

ANNA MARIA TAIGI

In 1840, Pope Gregory made Bishop Mastai a cardinal. Halfway through Mastai's tenure at Imola, Anna Maria Taigi

---

[4] Carlton H. Hayes, *The Historical Evolution of Modern Nationalism* (New York: Richard R. Smith, Inc., 1931), 151–154.
[5] Dillon, *Grand Orient Freemasonry Unmasked*, 50–51.
[6] Ibid., 65.
[7] See Bessières, S. J., *Wife, Mother and Mystic*, 235.

died in Rome. During the last years of her life "she beheld in the fullest detail the conspiracies of the secret societies, particularly as directed against the head of the Church and the superior ranks of the clergy."[8]

Taigi gave herself over to physical mortifications and penances so relentless they hastened her death. She became a victim soul in response to the frightening visions she saw in her sun: "Rome battered by revolution," millions dying "by the sword in war and civil strife, other millions in unforeseen death." Even worse were the spiritual chastisements:

> She saw the earth enveloped in flame; darkness covering it; immense edifices flung down; the earth and the heavens as it were in agony...She saw lightning, and in the midst of the lightning laymen falling into the abyss, [along with] ecclesiastical dignitaries and also priests and men and women of religious orders...
>
> (One day] she looked into her sun and saw the destiny of those who had died during that day. Very few, not as many as ten, went straight to heaven; many remained in purgatory, and those cast into hell were as numerous as flakes of snow in mid-winter."[9]

These visions, or prophecies, if you will, have a timeless quality like the Fatima apparitions. In 1823, Taigi saw Pope Gregory's successor. He was a young priest "now far beyond the seas." In fact Mastai was in Chile in 1823.

After accurately describing his physical appearance, Taigi foretold that Mastai would take the name Pius IX. She said "This gentle and benevolent pontiff will be favored by special light and guidance from heaven ... in the latter years of his life he will possess the gift of miracles..."[10]

---

[8] Edward Healy Thompson, M. A., *The Life of the Venerable Anna Maria Taigi, The Roman Matron*, (New York and Cincinnati: Pustet & Co., 1883, 304.
[9] Bessières, *Wife, Mother and Mystic*, 166–67, 178, 184–85.
[10] Rev. Richard Brennan, *Life of Pope Pius IX*, (New York: Benziger Brothers, 1878), 72–3.

According to Taigi, Pius IX was "singled out by heaven, and divinely commissioned to avert the storm which was soon to break, with apparently irresistible fury and power against the Bark of Peter." She foresaw that "after many and varied trials and humiliations, the Church shall achieve, before the eyes of the world, such a glorious triumph, that men will stand in silent awe and admiration."[11]

A NEW POPE

It was in 1846, nine years after Anna Maria's passing, that Pope Gregory came to the end of his life.

His last request was to "die like a monk" in sackcloth and ashes on a pallet in a simple cell. Gregory's monastic bent was reflected in his pontificate. He revitalized many religious orders and, perhaps because of the shambles the Revolution was making of Europe, greatly expanded mission work throughout the world.

These enduring accomplishments, and his absolute opposition to the Revolution, Freemasonry, and liberalism were the legacy Gregory bequeathed to his successor.

Given the continual political unrest in Rome and the Papal States, it was thought best to elect a new pope quickly. The conclave would begin before all the foreign cardinals arrived. Cardinal Mastai boarded a carriage and began a jolting, jarring trip on the rutted road to Rome.

On a hot, dusty day, Mastai stopped in the small market town of Fossombrone to rest from his bumpy ride. A crowd gathered and speculated about the upcoming conclave. Finally, Mastai blessed everyone and entered his carriage. A flash of white descended from the sky, and a white dove landed atop the carriage.

For the crowd, it was a sign from Heaven. Immediately shouts of "*Ecco il Papa! Viva il Papa!*" (Behold the Pope! Long Live the Pope!) pierced the hot summer air.[12] As the

---

[11] Ibid.
[12] John Gilmary Shea, *The Life of Pope Pius IX*, (New York: Thomas Kelly Publishers, 1877), 58.

carriage clattered away the dove remained perched on the roof. The crowd went home, their questions about the conclave answered.

Mastai missed the whole thing. An obscure cardinal still suspect at Rome for his alleged liberalism, Mastai was certain he would not be the next pope. Pope Gregory's secretary of state, Cardinal Lambruschini, was the favored candidate going into the conclave. Fifty-four cardinals began the conclave at the Quirinal Palace. Mastai was chosen to read the ballots during each round of voting, which would last until one candidate received thirty-six votes.

An impasse occurred almost immediately between the conservative and liberal blocs in the cardinalate. To break the deadlock, cardinals from both factions began voting for a compromise candidate not clearly aligned with either faction. At the final vote on the first day of the conclave Cardinal Mastai received twenty votes. Stunned and distraught, he spent the entire night in prayer. Having witnessed the crushing papal crosses of Pius VI and Pius VII, Mastai desired this particular chalice pass from his hands.

The next day, June 16, 1846, the new pope was elected. After the fourth ballot, Cardinal Mastai found himself repeatedly announcing his own name. His eyes blurred with tears, and his voice faltered. He begged to be excused from his role of reader, but this would have invalidated the voting. Collecting himself by prayer, he continued. Upon pronouncing his name for the thirty-sixth time, Mastai fell to his knees in prayer.

When asked if he accepted his election, he replied: "There are others more worthy than I am for the high office to which your Sacred College has called me. But as I have been long accustomed in Christ's service to yield up my own will, so now I accept that of God."[13]

In proof of his acceptance, he chose a name commemorating the suffering of his predecessors, and anticipating the

---

[13] O'Reilly, *A Life of Pius IX*, 79.

splinters of his own crosses. He would be known as Pius IX.

For a moment the new pope lost his composure and wept. Then he gathered himself and strode onto the balcony at the Quirinal Palace to give the waiting crowd his first blessing. A shout went up: "*Quanto e bello!*" How handsome he is!" Even an enemy would remark upon:

> ... the clear, musical voice of Mastai, whose name henceforth was to be absorbed into that of Pio Nono... the fair, comely face with a ray of beatified light upon it as his hand was uplifted to bless the tens of thousands in the Piazza below; a very God on earth he seemed for the moment, and as such to be worshipped on bended knee.[14]

But he was only a man, no matter how much the Revolution worships man instead of God. And when man is found wanting the worship ends and he is cannibalized in the name of progress and the rights of man.

Today the Revolution tries to destroy the memory of Blessed Pius IX. During his lifetime they tried to destroy his very person. His sins, in their eyes, were legion. Chief among them, perhaps, was Pius holding a mirror for all the world to see the true face of the Revolution, and it could not suffer the light he shone on its twisted visage.

o   o   o

Anna Maria Taigi's prophecies and the dove on Cardinal Mastai's carriage were not the only signs of grace heralding his ascension to the papacy. Thirty-three years prior to Mastai's 1846 election Pope Pius VII, imprisoned at Fontainebleau, entrusted a sealed packet to a servant. He instructed the packet be opened and read in 1846.

The servant died, and the packet was forgotten. In 1846 the servant's son chanced upon it. Inside was a written statement by Pius VII that the occupant of the episcopal chair in

---

[14] Frances Minto Elliot, *Roman Gossip*, (Leipzig: Bernhard Tauchnitz, 1896), 43.

Imola in 1846 would become Pope and would choose the name Pius IX.[15]

It was not clear from Pius VII's letter whether he knew Cardinal Mastai would be Pius IX. It is known that he took the future Pope Pius IX under his wing and prophesied the permanent curing of Mastai's epilepsy. How much more Pius VII knew about Pius IX is presently veiled by the inscrutable designs of Providence.

According to Taigi, Pius IX was "singled out by heaven, and divinely commissioned to avert the storm which was soon to break, with apparently irresistible fury and power against the Bark of Peter." She foresaw that "after many and varied trials and humiliations, the Church shall achieve, before the eyes of the world, such a glorious triumph, that men will stand in silent awe and admiration."[16]

---

[15] Brennan A. M., *Life of Pope Pius IX*, 73.
[16] Ibid.

. . . .

CHAPTER 5

THE *RISORGIMENTO*

I T was late at night when the priest made an unscheduled visit to the public hospital. No nurses or doctors were present. Moans of pain drew the priest to a patient's bedside. The two whispered together for a short time. The priest gave the stricken man *Viaticum*, and held him as he died.

The next morning, the same priest walked the streets of Rome as the sun rose. A homeless boy ran up to him. "Are you the Pope?" the boy asked. Pius nodded. "I have no father," the boy told him, and began to cry. "Then I will be a father to you," replied Pius IX. When an investigation confirmed the boy was telling the truth, Pius provided for his necessities and ensured he received a Christian education.[1]

Encounters like these were so routine even an enemy of Pius IX called him "the protector of all waifs, strays and orphans."[2] Twelve years later Pio Nono would provide a similar service for another boy, six-year-old Edgardo Mortara. With Edgardo, the price of fatherhood was heavy — some even claim it cost Pius the Papal States.

PIUS IX AND THE JEWS

The new pope traveled all around Rome, on foot and in coach. On a trip through Trastevere — the poor, mean streets of Rome — Pius noticed a crowd gathered around a fallen man. As Pius approached bystanders said, "Leave him alone, it's a Jew." "It is a man," replied Pius, "a suffering human creature who must be succoured (given aid)." What

---

[1] John Francis Maguire, M. P., *Pontificate of Pius the Ninth* (London: Longmans, Green, And Co., 1870), 30–32.
[2] Elliot, Elliot, *Roman Gossip*,58.

happened next was described not by a pious monk, but by
a political *enemy* of Pius IX:

> Tenderly raising the unfortunate Jew in his arms,
> he [Pius] placed him beside him, and drove him
> to his home, remaining with him until he became
> conscious, and sending afterwards his own physi-
> cian to attend him.[3]

The same enemy of Pius admitted, "One might multiply to any amount anecdotes of the benevolence of the
Pope."[4] Curious behavior, indeed, for someone whom
today's media calls an "extreme anti-semite."[5] Even more
curious was Pius IX's generous alms to Rome's Jews and
his permission for them to appoint a successor to their
high priest, who had died twelve years earlier. At the conclusion of the induction ceremony, the gathered Jews sang
a hymn of gratitude to Pius.[6] When he authorized Jews
to live outside the ghetto, and then razed the ghetto walls,
an exuberant rabbi proclaimed Pius IX the long-awaited
Messiah.[7]

None of these incidents were media events, photo oppor-
tunities, or grand symbolic gestures crafted for some glorious
ecumenical payoff. The kindness Pio Nono showed the Jews
he showed to all. His motive? To practice Christian charity
in imitation of Christ and in the hope of attracting souls
to Christ's Church. By a happy combination of God's grace
and his own natural gifts, Pius was so charitable even his
enemies appreciated him.

The new Pope also began a series of controversial political
and social reforms. The boldest move was the granting of
amnesty to all political prisoners in the Papal States, most
of whom were revolutionaries or criminals. This electrified

---

[3] Ibid., 57.
[4] Ibid.
[5] From *The Jerusalem Post*, September 5, 2000.
[6] Maguire, *Pontificate of Pius the Ninth*, 40.
[7] Daniel-Rops, *The Church in an Age of Revolution*, 240.

Italy and all of Europe. Freemasons Mazzini and Garibaldi publicly declared themselves supporters of the new Pope, and urged more reforms.

Privately, Mazzini ordered his followers to use every reform of Pius IX as an excuse to "assemble the masses, [even if] only to testify gratitude." These gatherings would "give the people the feeling of its strength, and render it more exacting."[8] Mazzini intended to use the mob as a lever to apply irresistible pressure on the new Pope. "We shall make him the fatted ox of politics," Mazzini declared of Pius IX. "We shall suffocate him with flowers."[9]

LA SALETTE

Far from frenzied Rome, flowers of a different sort dazzled the eyes of two young cowherds on a mountain in southern France. Less than three months after Pius IX became Pope the Blessed Virgin appeared to two children: fifteen-year-old Mélanie Calvat and eleven-year-old Maximin Giraud. The two had met only the day before while tending cows for different owners. Melanie did not wish to spend her time with Maximin but relented when the boy persisted.

The next day, Saturday, September 19, was sunny and cloudless. After eating lunch the children fell asleep. Melanie awoke to discover the cows were gone. She roused Maximin and they began retrieving the animals. Suddenly, Mélanie "saw a brightness like the sun." As they neared a small spring they saw "a Lady in the bright light; she was sitting with her head in her hands."[10]

She rose as the children approached. "Her clothing was silver-white and quite brilliant," Mélanie recalled. "It was made up of light and glory, sparkling and dazzling. There is no expression nor comparison to be found on earth." The tall, beautiful lady seemed all light and flowers:

---

[8] Maguire, *Pontificate of Pius the Ninth*, 36.
[9] Daniel-Rops, *The Church in an Age of Revolution*, 242.
[10] Right Reverend Ullathorne (Bishop of Birmingham), *The Holy Mountain of La Salette* (Hartford, CT: Fathers of La Salette, 1901), 47.

The crown of roses which She had placed on
Her head was so beautiful, so brilliant, that it
defies imagination. The different coloured roses
were not of this earth; it was a joining together
of flowers which crowned the head of the Most
Holy Virgin.

But the roses kept changing and replacing
each other, and then, from the heart of each
rose, there shone a beautiful entrancing light,
which gave the roses a shimmering beauty. From
the crown of roses there seemed to arise golden
branches and a number of other little flowers
mingled with the shining ones. The whole thing
formed a most beautiful diadem...[11]

The Lady's hands and hair were concealed, and the tears
that flowed from her eyes "vanished in the light like sparks."[12]
She reproached "her people" for their failure to pray, attend
Mass, and refrain from blasphemies they committed on Sun-
days. Saying that she had to pray for them continually to
avert God's wrath, the Lady asserted: "You will never be
able to make up for the trouble I have taken for you all!" She
foretold poor harvests for potatoes, corn, nuts, and grapes.
She said a famine would grip the land and that "children
under seven will begin to tremble and will die in the arms
of those who hold them."

Then she imparted secrets — first to Maximin, then to
Mélanie. She said if people converted the famine would end
and food would be plentiful. After admonishing the children
to pray more she passed again into heaven, repeating these
words: "And so, my children, you will pass this on to all my
people." They never saw her again, but Mélanie remembered
that "the last looks of the Blessed Virgin were mournfully
cast towards Rome."[13]

---

[11] Fr. Paul Gouin, *Sister Mary of the Cross, Shepherdess of La Salette* (New
Jersey: 101 Foundation), 73.
[12] *CRC*, no. 287 (July–August 1996): 4.
[13] Ullathorne, *The Holy Mountain of La Salette*, 126.

THE *RISORGIMENTO*

At that time, Rome contained most of the revolutionaries to whom Pius had granted amnesty, including Felice Orsini, who later tried to assassinate Napoleon III. They acted in concert with Mazzini (who operated from Paris because Italy had banned him) to inflame Italian nationalism and then exploit it for their own purposes. Mazzini shunned open debate on the Austrian occupation of parts of Italy as "neither necessary nor opportune." Instead, he encouraged the use of slogans to stir passions and numb intellects.

In October 1846, one month after the Blessed Virgin appeared at La Salette, Mazzini wrote his Roman operatives:

> There are regenerative words which contain all that need be often repeated to the people. 'Liberty, rights of man, progress, equality, fraternity', are what the people will understand, above all when opposed to the words despotism, privileges, tyranny, slavery, etc.... The essential thing is that the goal of the great revolution be unknown to them: Let us never let them see more than the first step.[14]

The "goal of the great revolution" of Giuseppe Mazzini was, according to the bylaws of *Young Italy*, "the indispensable destruction of all the Governments of the [Italian] peninsula" to "form a single State of all Italy in republican form."[15] To ensure secrecy the bylaws declared traitors were to be "poignarded without remission."[16] Those who escaped this fate were to be "pursued incessantly in every place; and the guilty shall be struck by an invisible hand, were he sheltered on the bosom of his mother, or in the tabernacle of Christ ..."[17]

---

[14] Maguire, *Pontificate of Pius the Ninth* 26–27.
[15] Ibid., 27.
[16] Ibid. A poignard is a long, lightweight thrusting knife with an acutely pointed blade.
[17] Ibid.

The public name for this Masonic conspiracy was the *Risorgimento* ("Revival"), also known as the *unification* of Italy. Today, it is portrayed as a popular national uprising. At the time, however, virtually no Italian outside the secret societies wished to turn Italy into a gigantic secular republic,[18] much less destroy the papal government and all the other regional governments on the Italian peninsula. Freemasonry was parasitic on Italian nationalism[19] and insidious through the extreme secrecy with which Mazzini cloaked his goals. Publicly, Mazzini proclaimed his allegiance to Pius IX; privately, he conspired for his downfall.

Shortly after becoming pope Pio Nono was given secret writings of the Illuminati group *Alta Vendita*, which contained none of the pleasing, high-sounding humanism of public Masonry. Instead, Pius read:

> Our ultimate end is that of Voltaire and of the French Revolution — the final destruction of Catholicism, and even of the Christian idea. The work we have undertaken is not the work of a day, nor of a month, nor of a year. It may last many years, a century, perhaps; in our ranks the soldier dies, but the fight goes on...
>
> Crush the enemy whoever he may be; crush the powerful by means of lies and calumny.... Make men's hearts corrupt and vicious, and you will no longer have Catholics. Draw away the priests from the altars, and from the practice of virtue. Strive to fill their minds and occupy their time with other matters...
>
> It is the corruption of the masses we have undertaken — the corruption of the people through the clergy, and of the clergy by us — the

---

[18] Patrick Keyes O'Clery, *The Making of Italy* (London: Kegan Paul, Trench, Trübner & Co., Ltd., 1892), 550–551. The author notes the *"Risorgimento"* is a myth. In fact, Italian "unification" was "the act of a party, helped by foreign arms, against the armed protests of whole districts of the country."

[19] As 20th century fascism would be under Mussolini.

corruption which ought one day to enable us to
lay the Church in the tomb.[20]

The essential first step for the *Risorgimento* to succeed
required the removal of Austrian troops from Italy. Only
then could the unification fully proceed. Masonic appeals
to Italian nationalism with slogans such as "Italy for the
Italians" unwittingly aligned many Italians with Masonry,
which exploited patriotism to drive the hated Austrians off
Italian soil.

Pius IX was as patriotic as any Italian. His patriotism
was mistaken for—and misrepresented as—sympathy for
the Revolution. In fact, Pius had no intention of ceding
the Papal States or his temporal power to any man-made
authority. He believed the States were a sacred trust he
must preserve to pass on to his successor. Thus, Pio Nono
became a force to be eliminated so progress could flow
unimpeded.

---

[20] Rev. E. Cahill, S.J., *Freemasonry and the Anti-Christian Movement*,
(Dublin: M. H. Gill and Son Ltd., 1949), 14.

• •

CHAPTER 6

THE NOOSE TIGHTENS

T HE Revolution was inexorably focusing its vision on Catholic Rome and Blessed Pius IX.

Mazzini's plan was to create a "Third Rome." There had been pagan Rome, and now there was Christian Rome. The god of progress, who spoke through the will of the people, would level Christian Rome and create a third Rome: Republican Rome.

For Mazzini the people were the interpreters of God's law, and God's law was Progress.[1] He envisioned far more than a change in government—he saw himself as the leader of a new religion, the *Faith of the Future*, which would unite all nations in a collective, glorious destiny. In short, Mazzini was the first to publicly champion a New World Order.

Mazzini instructed his agents in Rome: "Promise them [the clergy] liberty, and they will march in your ranks." Rulers and popes who passed progressive laws were to be praised, then pressured to go further: "Make equality penetrate the Church, and everything shall succeed...."

The people should be told "often, everywhere, and at length, of their misery and wants," Mazzini continued. "When a great number of associates, receiving the password with the command to spread an idea and make it public opinion, shall be able to concert a movement, they will find the old social edifice laid open on every side, and tumbling down, as if by miracle, at the first breath of Progress."[2]

---

[1] Hales, *Pio Nono*, 107.
[2] O'Reilly, *The Life of Pius IX*, 86–87.

QUI PLURIBUS

Pius IX's awareness of Mazzini's secret subversions is well documented through his private statements[3] and his first encyclical, *Qui Pluribus,* wherein he denounced "those secret sects who have come forth from the darkness to destroy and desolate both the sacred and the civil commonwealth."[4]

Describing "men who have become abominable in their pursuits," who "destroy faith on the pretext of human progress," Pio Nono essentially predicted the Roman Revolution by observing how secret societies "even trample underfoot the rights both of the sacred and of the civil power."[5]

The Pope then noted prior papal condemnations of Freemasonry and secret societies and declared: "We now confirm these [condemnations] with the fullness of Our Apostolic power."[6]

Pio Nono has been accused of being a stubborn antagonist of Italian aspirations to independence. In reality, he was a stubborn antagonist of *Masonic* aspirations. Part of the love affair between Pius and his people was their shared conviction that Italy must gain independence. How that would be done, and what would happen afterward, however, were the pressing questions.

Italy was a land of many regions and many different governments: Naples, Tuscany, the Papal States, Sicily, Piedmont, and the regions of northern Italy. Pius made several efforts to form a federation of Italian territories. Had events been allowed to proceed organically, it is likely the various Italian states would have eventually reached a preliminary agreement on joint government.

The problem for the Freemasons was that even if an Italian confederation were formed, many Italians preferred

---

[3] Daniel-Rops, *The Church in an Age of Revolution*, 241.
[4] Pope Pius IX, *Qui Pluribus*, November 9, 1846, para. 13 (Angelus Press edition), 1998.
[5] Ibid., paras. 12–13.
[6] Ibid., para 13.

Pio Nono to be its president.[7] Confederation leaders would have been shocked by the Masonic plan to impose a secular republic like that of the French Revolution. [8]

To simply wait for Italians to make up their minds would take entirely too long. Besides, they couldn't be trusted to make the right decision. Consequently, outside pressure had to be applied. Freemasons manipulated the passions of the time by magnifying the natural grievances and misunderstandings between Italy and the occupying Austrian army. The secret societies portrayed Pius IX as sympathetic to the Revolution—a leader who wished to lead a crusade against Austria but was blocked by his reactionary Curia and the "dastardly Jesuits."

REVOLUTIONS

Metternich predicted that in 1848, "many realities will have lifted from them the veils with which they are still covered.... The veil is liberalism. It will disappear in Italy, as in every other country, before radicalism in action."[9] This included a March revolution in Austria, from which Metternich himself had to flee.

Throughout 1848, revolutions toppled thrones across Europe, definitively ending the Congress of Vienna's initiative to maintain monarchical governments.[10] The northern Italian territory of Piedmont declared war on Austria. The press, secret societies, and revolutionary groups in Rome clamored for the Pope bless their efforts.

Most of Rome's new parliament either supported the Revolution or were too timid to oppose it. They, too pressured Pius to join Piedmont in declaring war on Austria. He refused, but in his duty as temporal sovereignhe dispatched

---

[7] This was Gioberti's proposal, which Pius declined.
[8] Piedmont, which was actually part of the larger Kingdom of Sardinia, sabotaged the efforts of Pius IX, Tuscany, and Naples to form an Italian confederation by refusing to meet with the other parties.
[9] Hales, *Pio Nono*, 68.
[10] Known as the Restoration.

troops[11] to the northern borders of the Papal States as a strictly defensive measure. The leader, General Durando, conspired with the Piedmontese to betray Pius.

A Piedmontese agent gave Durando a document the general published to his troops, falsely claiming Pius IX had blessed their aggression against Austria. The document specified that troops be decorated with the cross of Christ and that their battle cry be "God wills it!"[12]

Durando was not the first to align Pius IX with violent Italian nationalism in an attempt to force the Pope to bless the Revolution. But the timing of his ploy and his utter disobedience — he marched far north of the Papal States and did battle with the Austrians, falsely maintaining this was Pius' will — raised the stakes considerably.

Piedmont thought Pius would concede Durando's disobedience as a *fait accompli*. Mazzini's Italian Masons created the illusion that Durando's actions meant Pio Nono blessed the Masonic unification plot. This artfully dovetailed with prior revolutionary propaganda that the Pope supported the Revolution but was being thwarted by dark forces in the Curia.

STONE OF CONTRADICTION

It is clear from his correspondence with the Grand Duke of Tuscany that Pius IX understood the situation. The Pope had been

> The first to perceive the poison concealed beneath the veil of religion in such schemes; no one was more certain than himself that, once the agitators of this type had obtained their desire, the sovereignty of the [papal] Tiara would be thrown to the earth even sooner than that of any other monarchy, and banished from the scene.[13]

---

[11] Made up of the Civic Guard and a newly formed National Guard.
[12] O'Reilly, *A Life of Pius IX*, 191–192.
[13] Hales, *Pio Nono*, 75–76 (report of Tuscany ambassador).

The showdown had finally arrived, and Pius IX would not blink first. His allocution of April 29, 1848, emphatically separated the Pope from his renegade general's hostilities against Austria. He then explained why he could not support military aggression against Austria:

> Unworthy though we be, we hold on earth the place of Him who is the author of peace and the lover of charity, embracing as we do, in fulfillment of our apostolic charge, all countries and peoples and nationalities in one undivided sentiment of fatherly love.[14]

Finally, he vigorously urged Italians to shun Mazzini's plans for a unified Italy. The Church was the true — nay, only — source of unity. Thus, Pius IX set his face like flint against the spirit of the age. As all Popes must do, he resisted seemingly irresistible tides pressuring him to forsake the City of God for the City of Man.

In one fell swoop, Pius punctured the liberal-Masonic illusion of Pio Nono, *Patriot-Pope*; unflinchingly laid bare the ambitions of his enemies; and urged all to seek refuge in, and guidance from, the Church. Pius IX had steered the barque of Peter sharply away from the shoals of the revolution.

The Pope's stand was a remarkable act of apostolic courage. He would never be forgiven for this by his contemporaries — or by what passes for modern history.

The Palm Sunday of Pius IX's pontificate was over. The passion of Pius IX had begun.

---

[14] Pope Pius IX, *Allocution of April 29, 1848*, delivered in a secret consistory.

. . . .

CHAPTER 7

THE ROMAN REVOLUTION

B
Y the summer of 1848 the campaign of "Italy for the Italians" was in shambles. The Austrians routed the Piedmontese armies, regained control of northern Italy, and forced "The Sword of Italy," Piedmontese King Charles Albert, to sign an armistice.

Charles had supported the war urged by his liberal government in an attempt to save his crown, but his support only purchased a few scant months. After signing the armistice King Charles abdicated the throne to his son, Victor Emmanuel, thus becoming the first official scapegoat for the failure of the *Risorgimento*.

Unwilling to admit defeat, Rome's new Parliament passed a measure allowing the drafting of civilians and the use of several hundred thousand dollars to jump-start the war effort. Pius IX firmly vetoed the proposals.

The Pope's strong public disapproval deflated the enthusiasm of Durando's army, who eventually felt silly wearing crosses and declaring "God wills it" when their Pope so obviously disagreed with them. More effective with rhetoric than weaponry, Durando's army was pushed around until they finally left northern Italy and returned, sulking, to Rome.

In short order the second official scapegoat for the failed campaign was elected: the once beloved Pio Nono. The new party line issuing from the lodges of *Young Italy* targeted the passions of disillusioned nationalists who had believed the Masonic fairy tale of "Patriot-Pope Pio Nono."

Now they were told: Hadn't Mazzini warned them not to trust princes and rulers? Now even Pius IX had betrayed Italy. It was time for the "will of the people" to assert itself.

Those who had once virtually deified Pius IX now condemned him as "the enemy of his country" and a "friend of despots."[1] They might as well have called him a Jesuit; the Society, however, had left Rome months earlier at the behest of Pius IX, who feared for their safety.

To ensure Pius would not follow suit, the Civic Guard—now an instrument of the Revolution—posted guards on all roads leaving Rome and began spying on prelates and clergy.

THE ROSSI ASSASSINATION

Pius was aware of the discontent. "Our words have excited a commotion which threatens to break out into open violence," the Pope observed. Then, as if foreseeing the future—and perhaps seeing Rome through the same mournful eyes as the Virgin of La Salette—he exclaimed:

> Save, O Lord, your Rome from so many evils!
> Enlighten those who will not listen to the voice of
> your vicar! Let wiser counsels prevail with all, so
> that, obedient to those who govern them, they may
> live in the exercise of the duties of good Christians.[2]

Having failed to unify Italy, the Revolution decided to tear apart Rome. Crime and violence increased. Political agitation for a lay Minister of State led to intolerable conditions for a string of ministers appointed by Pius, all of whom resigned. The Pope finally appointed a lay minister, but his choice of Count Pellegrino Rossi temporarily checkmated the agitators.

For most of his life, Rossi had been a political revolutionary, but by the time of Pius' appointment, Rossi's earlier faith had been restored. Now a firm Catholic, Rossi used his understanding of the Revolution to put a spoke in the wheel of the Revolution.

He restricted public meetings used to agitate the masses. He jailed the revolutionary monk Gavazzi, who was preaching violent rebellion against the Pope. Rossi censored the revolutionary press and used his ministry as a bully pulpit to publicize the true goals of the Revolution.

---

[1] Brennan, *Life of Pope Pius IX*, 146.
[2] Maguire, *Pontificate of Pius the Ninth*, 53.

Minister Rossi was definitely *not* the layman *Young Italy* had been pining for. In the spirit of liberty, equality, and fraternity, the Revolution decreed Rossi a traitor to the cause — a charge punishable by death. The sentence was to be administered by stabbing Rossi in the neck until he was dead.

Under a surgeon's direction, aspiring assassins practiced their thrusts on a corpse procured from a local hospital. On the morning of November 15, 1848, Rossi was stabbed to death on the steps outside the Parliament building.

That night a raucous parade carried the still-bloody knife aloft in triumph amid cries of "Blessed be the hand that killed Rossi!"[3] The mob paused outside Rossi's apartment to serenade his grieving wife and young daughter with a taunting *Miserere* (Psalm 50). Was this really the will of the people?

MOB RULE

After the parade, Galletti, Sterbini, and Ciceruacchio organized troops from Durando's army and distributed guns and ammunition. At daybreak Galletti and Sterbini — the new self-appointed leaders of Rome's constitutional government — marched on the Quirinal Palace at the head of a band-playing, rifle-toting mob shouting *Viva la Repubblica!* and "Death to the priests!"

The armed mob outside numbered over one thousand. Inside the palace were a few dozen Swiss Guards. Pio Nono "was walking up and down, calm, even serene, but entirely deserted except by the foreign ambassadors and a few servants."[4] Cardinal Antonelli also remained. His loyalty would never be forgotten by Pius.

Sterbini and Galletti, who had been granted amnesty by Pius IX, now repaid this favor by giving Pius a face-to-face ultimatum. He had one hour to agree to give up his temporal

---

[3] O'Reilly, *A Life of Pius IX*, 222. See also Hales, *Pio Nono*, 89–90. It is highly probable that Sterbini and Ciceruacchio planned Rossi's murder, although neither was convicted at a trial years later. It was later proved that Ciceruacchio's son, Luigi Brunetti, delivered the fatal blow.

[4] Hales, *Pio Nono*, 92.

power and declare war on Austria, or the mob would storm the Quirinal.

Pius told Sterbini and Galletti he would consider their demands. The two began arguing with the Pope. Pius replied that he would not be coerced. Nor would he abdicate. The ultimatum would reduce him to a functionary, allowing him only to "pray and to bless." He preferred martyrdom.[5]

Surprised Pius did not concede to their demands, Sterbini and Galletti left the Quirinal. The Swiss Guard immediately barricaded all entrances to prevent a rush on the palace doors. Unable to force entry, the mob strafed the Quirinal with gunfire.

Pius' secretary, Bishop Palma, was killed instantly by a bullet to the head. Several of the Pope's personal staff were wounded. Bullets began entering Pius' anteroom. Cannons were trained on the Quirinal doors, and scaling ladders were positioned to storm the Papal Palace.

A truce was declared. The revolutionary delegation reentered the Quirinal and repeated their demands. They threatened that Pius' refusal would result in the storming of the Quirinal and the deaths of all inside, "with the sole exception of the Pontiff himself."[6]

Realizing his presence could no longer safeguard his allies, Pius gathered the diplomatic corps to witness his solemn protest:

> "Look where we stand," the Pope declared. "There is no hope in resistance. Already a prelate is slain in my very palace. Shots are aimed at it, artillery leveled. We are pressed and besieged by the insurgents. To avoid fruitless bloodshed and more heinous enormities, we give way, but, as you see, gentlemen, it is only to force. So we protest...all we concede is invalid, is null, is void."[7]

---

[5] Ibid.
[6] Lillian Browne-Olf, *Their Name Is Pius* (Milwaukee: Bruce Publishing Company, 1941), 177.
[7] O'Reilly, *A Life of Pius IX*, 229.

Galletti waved to the mob from a Quirinal balcony and shouted, "The sovereign has given us a republic!"[8] In return the revolutionary leaders replaced the loyal Swiss Guard with the traitorous Civic Guard. Formed by the Pope to safeguard public order against revolutionary subversion, the Civic Guard had themselves been subverted. Now they were the Revolution's jailers, and Pio Nono was their prisoner of war.

Under these conditions it was impossible for Pius to direct the affairs of the Church. Yet he remained, thinking his presence might avert further bloodshed. Besides, it was clear he was not free to leave.

He had no intention of consenting to the Revolution's demands and was content with martyrdom — until he received a sign. The Bishop of Valence gave Pius a small silver container used by Pius VII to conceal a particle of a Host during his exile from Rome. Pius IX took this as a sign from Heaven that he too was to enter exile.

ESCAPE

The Pope's last official act in Rome took place on November 24, 1848. He met with the revolutionary leaders of the new Roman government, refused to agree to their plans, and returned to his room. Guards stood outside his door. Sentries were posted around the interior of the Quirinal Palace. Spies roamed both the interior and exterior of the palace.

It was dark when the French minister, the Duke d'Harcourt, pulled up to the Quirinal, stating he had urgent business to discuss immediately with the Pope. He was allowed entry to Pius' apartment, and an escape plan went into effect.

D'Harcourt began reading aloud from newspapers to create the impression of a conversation for any listening ears. Meanwhile the Pope changed clothes in the next room. Pius' valet, Filippani, who had followed him from Imola, helped the Pope change from his white papal vestments to the simple cassock of a priest. Next, Pius secured on his

---

[8] Ibid.

person the small silver-gilt pyx that Pius VII used to secure a small portion of the Blessed Sacrament.

Over the cassock Filippani clothed the Pope in a dark overcoat, and a broad woolen neckcloth outside his priest's collar. Next came a low-brimmed hat and dark-tinted glasses. The Pope bore it all patiently, but when Filippani handed him a fake mustache and beard Pius refused: "No, I won't use those. They are ridiculous."[9]

After blessing an emotional d'Harcourt, Pius exited through a secret passageway with Filippani. All went well until the two reached the locked outside door and realized Filippani had forgotten the key. Leaving the Pope in darkness, the valet scurried back to retrieve it. Upon his return Filippani found Pius on his knees adoring the Blessed Sacrament reserved in the silver pyx.

The rusty door lock had not been used in years. Filippani feverishly worked the key in the lock. At first, the inner gears did not move, and the key almost snapped off. Finally the door slowly creaked open, and Pius stepped into a little-used courtyard. He climbed into a waiting coach that quietly clopped through Roman backstreets until it met a second coach.

This second coach contained the Bavarian diplomat Count Spaur, who transported Pius, disguised as a doctor, past patrols of Civic Guards and various checkpoints. At times Pius' passengers expressed fear they would be caught. The Pope reassured them: "Be calm," he said, "God is with us. I carry the Blessed Sacrament on my person."[10]

Finally, the second coach left Rome behind, and at a brisk trot headed south to the town of Gaeta in Naples.[11]

---

[9] O'Reilly, *A Life of Pius IX*, 229–238.

[10] Mark Fellows, *The Ninth Pius: The Last Pope-King* (Minneapolis: Remnant Press, 1996), 19–20.

[11] "Pope Pius IX Escapes from the Quirinal, November 24, 1848," *Catholic Textbook Project*, https://www.catholictextbookproject.com/post/pope-pius-ix-escapes-from-the-quirinal-november-24-1848

CHAPTER 8

. . . .

THE ROMAN REPUBLIC

PIUS IX reappeared in Gaeta, a small coastal town south of Rome in Naples. In public, the Roman revolutionaries proclaimed their great good news: "The Pope has fled — the papacy is at an end."[1]

Privately, however, there was much gnashing of teeth and frustration over the Pope having outsmarted them. For all their hatred of the Church and the papacy, the revolutionaries preferred to keep Pius in Rome, where they could manipulate him into blessing their cause — or at least create the illusion of papal approval.

But not only had Pio Nono disappeared from under their very noses, he had also taken the great seal with him, meaning no legislation passed by the Revolution had the force of law. Adding insult to injury, the Pope then formally closed the Roman Parliament.

Pius' fate dismayed and shocked Europe, including some Protestants willing to give the "liberal" pope the benefit of the doubt.[2] Even former allies of the Revolution turned a critical eye to the takeover of Rome. As we say today, it was not a good look.

What was a poor revolution to do? They sent delegations to Gaeta to persuade Pius to return to Rome. The Pope, however, refused to receive them. There were good reasons the Revolution preferred to work behind the scene. Pius' flight had thrust the Revolution into the spotlight and, as is invariably the case, its leaders revealed the sizable gap between their spoken ideals and their actual behavior.

---

[1] Maguire, *Pontificate of Pius the Ninth*, 67.
[2] The Protestant King of Prussia offered Pius a German castle as a haven.

THE ROMAN REPUBLIC IN ACTION

Many English-speaking historians maintain the Roman Revolution was tamer than the French Revolution, implying an evolution had taken place. Yes, it was now a kinder, gentler revolution—one that stole governments, destroyed churches, and murdered innocent people.

It is true that, unlike the French Revolution, the Roman Revolution did not result in the martyrdom and massacre of thousands of Catholics.[3] And thanks to the escape of Pius IX, it did not involve the murder of a sovereign like the French king (and queen).

Moreover, unlike the French Revolution, there is no evidence that the leaders of the Roman Republic engaged in or abetted cannibalism, necrophilia, and other depravities—that so scandalized the wife of a minister of the new French Republic, who in 1789 wrote:

> If only you knew the hideous details of the killings! Women brutally violated before being torn to pieces by those tigers, intestines cut out and worn as turbans; bleeding human flesh devoured.... You know my enthusiasm for the Revolution; Well, I am ashamed of it.[4]

So the bar of comparison is set extremely low—almost on the ground.[5] To the relief of its citizens the Roman Republic lasted less than a year. What was it like?

The gentlest way to describe it is: it was ironic. There was irony in the pleas for peace and patience from the new rulers—who only days before had impatiently disturbed the peace by directing an armed revolt, murdering innocent people, and imprisoning a pope.

And it was ironic that upon becoming rulers, the champions of a free press immediately suppressed all unfavorable

---

[3] There are conflicting casualty counts. It is safe to say deaths were at least in the high hundreds.
[4] Daniel-Rops, *The Church in an Age of Revolution*, 20.
[5] So low only Stalinism or Maoism could slither underneath.

press. A further irony was the Revolution's solemn vow to honor the will of the people, while in reality it imported foreign revolutionaries to dictate to the Romans what their will was. An additional importation of foreign mercenary soldiers was used to enforce this so-called will.

Sometimes the will of the people was to flee the new republic. But this will was not respected by the Revolution. Romans caught fleeing Rome were turned back, beaten, even killed. A Dominican priest leaving Rome to administer last rites was stabbed and killed in broad daylight by government secretary Antonio Zambianchi.[6]

THE NEW RULER

Sterbini and Galletti formed the Supreme Junta of Public Safety[7] and issued a decree for the democratic election of the representatives who would form the new republic.

An election of sorts occurred throughout Rome and the Papal States in February 1849. The populace stayed away in record numbers. In Pius' birthplace of Sinigaglia, only 200 out of 27,000 voted. In Rome, many cast their vote for Pope Pius IX or for Saint Peter. According to a neutral British navy commander present at the time, the will of the people was not to participate in or welcome a change in government. Instead "there was a nearly universal desire for the Pope's return."[8]

With the next day's dawn came a joyous proclamation of the victory of the will of the people: they now had the new government they had longed for.

The majority of the new Constituent Assembly were Freemasons, radicals, and assorted revolutionaries. Romans were informed Mazzini had received an overwhelming number of votes and would head the new Roman Republic. The first act of the new government was to depose Pope Pius IX.

---

[6] O'Reilly, *A Life of Pius IX*, p. 287.
[7] Yes, really.
[8] Hales, *Pio Nono*, p. 96.

Then Rome's new leader, Giuseppe Mazzini, arrived in Rome under the pretext he had been elected ruler. A more blatant lie regarding "the will of the people" is difficult to conceive, but audacity was the coin of the realm. Many non-Romans held high positions in the new republic, causing some Romans to wonder whose will was really being served. The answer came quickly.

Unfortunately for the Romans, Mazzini was a far better conspirator than administrator. His government spent its short existence stealing as much money and property as it could. Forced "loans" to the government were imposed on those deemed wealthy. Property owners were required to pay their taxes a year in advance. The government confiscated all bank accounts. The new republic celebrated its twelfth day of existence by declaring, on February 21, 1849: "All ecclesiastical property of the Roman States is the property of the Republic."[9]

Churches were plundered. Bells were taken from steeples and recast as cannons. Sacred vessels were melted down. Monasteries were converted into jails for "political prisoners." Church buildings became Masonic lodges. Other religious dwellings were used as tenement houses. Statues were mutilated or destroyed. Reliquaries were rifled. The catacombs were desecrated by adding piles of animal bones to the bones of the martyrs of the early Church.[10]

Not even the Holy House of Loreto, where a young Giovanni Mastai-Ferretti had prayed so fervently to the Blessed Virgin for the cure of his epilepsy, was exempt. The altar offerings left at Loreto (and at many other churches) by countless pious pilgrims were seized "In the Name of God and the People."

THE "NEW PASCH"

A nadir of sorts occurred when Mazzini unveiled a new liturgy for Easter 1849. Unable to obtain a regular priest, he

---

[9] Brennan, *Life of Pope Pius IX*, 168.
[10] Shea, *The Life of Pope Pius IX*, 162.

settled for the excommunicated monk Gavazzi. Aside from a few curious Romans, most in attendance were the reigning celebrities: Mazzini, his new government, and assorted radicals. Also present was the ambassador of the United States — the only foreign diplomat to remain in Rome after Pius' departure.

The service was called a "Requiem for the Dead Papacy."[11] Among other irregularities, military music replaced Gregorian chant. After the service, Gavazzi and Mazzini stepped onto a balcony festooned with banners of the new republic. There Gavazzi blessed the people while holding a host in his hand. Then Mazzini graced the crowd with a few well-chosen words about the Religion of the People.

What happened here? A "wicked profanation?"[12] A misguided attempt to placate the people with the religion they were used to?[13] Or a stab at a brand-new religion?[14] Mazzini called it the "New Pasch." Other than similar irregular services, there were very few public Masses to be found in Rome, not even on feast days.[15] Instead, the Blessed Sacrament was taken from altars and publicly ridiculed in the streets. In churches, hosts were ceremonially trampled.

These behaviors were eerily similar to those of the French Revolution and would be repeated in detail decades later by Communists. Although host desecration may have been political theater, it also mirrored rituals in black magic. To evoke the prince of this world or render him homage, one is required to "profane the ceremonies of the religion to which one belongs and to trample its holiest symbols underfoot."[16]

---

[11] Brennan, *Life of Pope Pius IX*, 169.
[12] Maguire's conclusion.
[13] Hales' conclusion.
[14] Author's conclusion.
[15] Hales, *Pio Nono*, 123–124.
[16] Nesta H. Webster, *Secret Societies and Subversive Movements* (London: Boswell Publishing Company Ltd., 1936), 246.

THE *FINANZIERI*

The previously mentioned Antonio Zambianchi was the leader of the *Finanzieri*,[17] a group of assassins who specialized in murdering priests. The half-buried bodies of fourteen priests were found outside Zambianchi's headquarters at the convent of San Callisto in Rome. Ninety more priests were found completely buried on convent grounds. These were not the only casualties of the new republic.

Contemporary apologists for Mazzini generally admit things got a little out of hand in Rome but claim much of the mayhem either occurred before Mazzini arrived or after he arrived but without his knowledge or consent. The mayhem included the murders of priests, host desecrations, and the destruction of religious property — all of which were commonplace.[18]

Obviously, Mazzini cannot be blamed for every theft, murder, and sacrilege committed during the (mercifully) short tenure of the Roman Republic. On the other hand, it is a documented fact that Mazzini controlled the Roman Revolution through his Masonic *Young Italy*, an organization that included many of the leading revolutionaries in Rome. Today, *Young Italy* might be considered a terrorist group, and Mazzini directed it.

As for the *Finanzieri*, it appears Mazzini was more than familiar with Zambianchi, penning an affectionate letter to him requesting "twenty other *finanzieri* to complete important operations." He signed the missive: "Thine, Giuseppe Mazzini."[19] After the Revolution was expelled from Rome, 250 priests were dead or missing.[20] Farini, a moderate member of the republic's government, spoke of live burials and other "unrepeatable horrors."[21]

---

[17] Translates as financier, or capitalist. Most likely an ironic reference.
[18] This is generally admitted, even by English-speaking historians.
[19] O'Reilly, *A Life of Pius IX*, 288.
[20] Ibid.
[21] Hales, *Pio Nono*, 122.

Writing in 1870, John Maguire, after giving examples of the "public butchery" of suspected Jesuits and noting "a long list of atrocious murders" committed during the reign of the Roman Republic, further observed:

> Notwithstanding their affectation of respect for religion, the government made no successful effort to check the fury...which lost no opportunity of inflicting injury upon the priests. While hymns of liberty were sung, and greetings of brotherhood were exchanged, dwellings were broken into, villas were plundered, property was appropriated, and every opportunity was availed of for violence or rapine.
>
> No doubt the government desired, and in many instances made attempts to restrain this lawlessness; but what could it do against numbers — especially against those who had been too well taught the lesson of their "strength"?[22]

---

[22] Maguire, *Pontificate of Pius the Ninth*, 91–92.

CHAPTER 9

ENTER THE IMMACULATE

S O the Revolution and Mazzini had Rome, and Pius IX seemed the picture of defeated futility in Gaeta. Less than two years later, however, Pius would be back in Rome and Mazzini would be "unceremoniously clapped into the prison-fortress of Gaeta."[1] Though it normally only rains on the just and unjust alike, history is capable of a rough sort of justice now and then.

Certainly Austria's Prince Metternich saw a rough justice served on the reforming pope, Pio Nono, whose liberal antics — as Metternich saw it — gave the Revolution all the ammunition it needed to topple the papal government and drive the Pope from Rome. But there would prove to be many layers and levels to the pontificate of Blessed Pius IX, and Metternich may have leapt too quickly at what he saw as cause and effect.

He was right that Pius' reforms provided cover for liberals and Freemasons. But it is also proper to consider the forces of Italian nationalism, Austrian (and French) foreign policy, the secularizing influence of the press, and the rise of Communism and Socialism.

Secular historians are in general agreement that all these natural forces influenced the pontificate of Pius IX — except for the role of Freemasonry, which they tend to minimize or ignore completely.

Also swept under the rug is the supernatural character of the Roman Catholic Church. The idea that God — and the devil — interact in the affairs of the world, that they wrestle for the souls of human beings, that religion is the impetus

---

[1] William Halperin, *Italy and the Vatican at War* (Chicago: University of Chicago Press, 1939), 28.

for life and death, for war and peace, for the rise and fall of nations — this is all dismissed by the makers of history as either superstition or lacking in objectivity, as if excluding God from history is being objective rather than being mistaken.

Many English-speaking historians either deny or do not seem to comprehend that religious history is *true* history, including the centuries-long belief that the Church, not historians, is the guardian of all the truth needed to save the eternal soul of every man, woman and child who has ever or will ever be born. For Christians, the only history since the Incarnation that truly matters is salvation history.

The history of the pontificate of Pope Pius IX began not at his election in 1846, or even at the Incarnation, but in *Genesis*, when God told the serpent: "I will place enmities between thee and the woman, and thy seed and her seed: she shall crush thy head, and thou shalt lie in wait for her heel."[2]

From his childhood Pius had a special veneration for the Mother of God. Proof of their bond was his petition to her for relief from his epilepsy and his subsequent permanent cure. Thus, there could only be enmity between Pius and the Revolution, which lay in wait to trap and destroy him, and through him, her.

To move from generalities to specifics, Metternich was only partly right about Pius and the Roman Revolution. The timing of the revolution's deadly attack against Pius IX had everything to do, I believe, with his intention of exalting the Blessed Virgin Mary by defining as dogma the Church's teaching on her Immaculate Conception.

Were Mazzini and the Revolution aware that in June 1848, as Pius' phenomenal popularity plummeted, the Pope appointed a commission of theologians to study the opportuneness of defining as dogma the doctrine of Mary's Immaculate Conception? Probably not. Even if they were aware, neither Mazzini nor his comrades would have attached the proper significance to Pius' intentions.

---

[2] Gen. 3:15

Yet perhaps the alarm was sounded at the supernatural level, and the hatred and fearful urgency of the prince of this world penetrated his agents and agencies. The result was a redoubled effort to destroy the papacy and papal power — that terrible power that can bind and loose, that awful strength that could truly exalt on earth what was exalted in Heaven; the Immaculate Virgin Mary.

The supernatural goal of the Roman Revolution was to destroy Pius IX, who was prudently, methodically moving towards a solemn definition of the Immaculate Conception. Since most — hopefully all — of the revolutionaries were not *conscious* agents of Lucifer, the supernatural aspect of the battle was off their radar.

Nevertheless, Lucifer scripted their actions as surely as Pio Nono acted in response to the urging of Heaven. Lucifer was not physically present with the mob firing on the Quirinal, but his spirit abided.

CHAPTER 10

PRONOUNCING THE IMMACULATE CONCEPTION

PIUS IX stayed disguised after arriving in Gaeta on November 25. He was met there by Secretary of State Cardinal Antonelli. They spent the night in a rundown hotel, waiting for King Ferdinand of Naples to respond to Pius' request for asylum. In his letter Pius expressed willingness to travel on if his presence in Naples was politically inconvenient.

The Pope's request was answered the next morning when three frigates docked in Gaeta's harbor. King Ferdinand and his entire court disembarked, seeking Pius' whereabouts, This caused confusion, as the Gaetans had no idea Pius was in town. Eventually, the Pope was found and taken to Gaeta's Royal Pavilion.

He appeared as calm, dignified, and friendly as if he were granting Ferdinand an audience in Rome. Overcome, the King and Queen of Naples knelt before him. Their wordless act of fealty broke the tension, and the royal court erupted with joy that Pope Pius IX was alive and unharmed, and with grief at the evil fate that had befallen him.

Ferdinand invited Pius to his royal castle to stay as long as he wished. In the coming weeks, the entire diplomatic corps (except for the American minister) and a good number of cardinals and prelates would reside in Gaeta.

Then came the mail. From all over the world, telegrams and letters from rulers and statesmen, and from religious and lay Catholics, poured into Gaeta. All expressed sympathy for the Pope and outrage over his fate.

EXILE AT GAETA

As for Blessed Pius IX, his first official act was *not* to
ask the Catholic powers to restore him to Rome. Pius did
not hold councils of war and diplomatic strategy either.
Instead, only days after arriving at Gaeta (December 6) he
"accelerated the process that would lead to the definition of
the dogma of the Immaculate Conception" by consulting
cardinals on the issue.[1]

On their recommendation, Pius issued, on February 2,
1849, the letter *Ubi Primum* to the world episcopate, asking
for their opinion on the proposed definition[2] and declaring:

> We have especial confidence in our hope that the
> Blessed Virgin—who has been elevated "by the
> greatness of Her merits high above all the choirs
> of angels and even unto the very throne of God"
> (Saint Gregory), who has crushed under the feet
> of Her virtues the head of the ancient serpent...
>
> And who, "placed between Christ and His
> Church" (Saint Bernard), full of grace and sweet-
> ness, has always delivered the Christian people
> from the greatest calamities and from the snares
> and assaults of all their enemies...
>
> ...will likewise deign to take pity on us and,
> with that immense tenderness so characteristic of
> Her maternal Heart, deliver us, through Her insis-
> tent and efficacious intercession with God, from
> the sad and pitiful misfortunes, the cruel anguish,
> the sorrows and needs from which we suffer...
>
> And deflect the punishments of God's anger
> which afflicts us on account of our sins, calm and
> disperse the terrible hurricanes of evil which assail
> the Church on every side to the immense sorrow
> of our soul, and finally turn our grief into joy.[3]

---

[1] *CRC*, September 2000, 16.
[2] Daniel-Rops, *The Church in an Age of Revolution*, 256. Of 603 responses,
546 urged the definition. Those few who did not questioned the opportuneness of the definition. Pius' exile may also have caused hesitation.
[3] Pius IX, *Ubi Primum*, December 2, 1849, Papal Encyclicals Online,

It was not until later that month, on February 18, that Pius formally asked the Catholic powers of Europe to restore the papacy to Rome. The Catholic powers were divided about how best to do this. By summer Napoleon III, under pressure from outraged French Catholics, sent an army to evict the Revolution and its international army from Rome. This was accomplished on July 3, 1849.

That fall, the Holy Father visited a church in Naples. After lingering in a small chapel dedicated to the Immaculate, he left a small, handwritten note: "Pius IX declares that he places himself under the protection of Mary Immaculate."[4]

THE RETURN TO ROME

The Roman Revolution left anarchy in its wake, delaying Pius' return to Rome until April 12, 1850. Once back, he resumed his plan to restore the hierarchy in England, also known as *Our Lady's Dowry*. This was formally announced on September 30, to a storm of anti-papal invective from England that rivaled the mob outside the Quirinal.

The restoration of the hierarchy in *Our Lady's Dowry* proved immensely fruitful. In less than a century, the number of English Catholics increased from one million to three million.[5] Pius' pontificate witnessed the public conversions of noted Englishmen — Newman, Faber, and Henry Edward Manning. All three would profess in touching terms their devotion to the Blessed Virgin.

The following year, Pius asked to see the secrets of La Salette. In the five years since the Blessed Virgin's appearance there, her woeful prophecies had come true — and not just in France.

Within a year of the Lady's appearance, Ireland was decimated by an historic potato famine. Potatoes, grapes, and nuts were important crops in the region of La Salette. They

https://www.papalencyclicals.net/Pius09/p9ubipr2.htm
[4] *CRC*, September 2000, 16
[5] Hales, *Pio Nono*, 141–142.

all failed, just as the Lady had warned. French papers of the time reported yearly deaths due to starvation in the tens of thousands, as well as an "unusual increase" in the mortality of small children in the Diocese of Grenoble, which contained La Salette.[6]

On July 18, 1851, Pius read the secrets entrusted by Mary to Maximin and Mélanie. Mélanie's secret caused visible emotion in the Pope. He paused, then said, "I must reread this with a calm head." When finished, the Holy Father declared, "France is threatened with scourges . . . the whole of Europe is culpable and deserves to be chastised . . . It is not for nothing that the Church is called militant, and here"—Pius touched his chest with his hand—"you behold its captain."[7]

PRONOUNCING THE IMMACULATE CONCEPTION

Three years later, the captain of the Church Militant issued a clarion call that resounded like a hammer blow from heaven. On December 8, 1854, Blessed Pius IX declared as dogma this teaching:

> That the most Blessed Virgin Mary, in the first instant of Her conception, by a singular grace and privilege granted by Almighty God, in view of the merits of Christ Jesus, the Savior of the human race, was preserved free from all stain of original sin . . .

There were over forty thousand in St. Peter's, yet there was no straining to hear the unamplified voice of Pius IX ringing like honey and thunder throughout the huge basilica.

As he finished, "tears rained down my cheeks," he confided later, for "God made me see so clearly and fully the incomparable purity of the Blessed Virgin that my soul

---

[6] See Ullathorne, *The Holy Mountain of La Salette*, 98–100. French secular papers estimated that in a three-year period after La Salette, 250,000 died of starvation.

[7] As quoted in *CRC*, July–August 96, 8, and Ullathorne, 125.

was overwhelmed with joy beyond this earth." Pius insisted that only God's grace prevented him from "dying of love through this knowledge, and the tremendous flood of exalted feeling."[8]

The relationship between Blessed Pius IX and the Blessed Virgin Mary only deepened during the next twenty-four years of his pontificate. So too did the hatred of the world and the fury of hell. Between them, they would strip Pius of everything but his faith.

o   o   o

Many of the bishops in Rome for the definition of the Immaculate Conception were amazed by the pope's small room. There was a narrow bed, a modest desk, and some sofas for guests. The uncarpeted floor contained loose floor bricks Pius warned his guests to avoid.

As pope, Pius earned approximately $5,000 a year. It is estimated he gave $1,000,000 annually in alms and other charitable contributions. His personal poverty, love of beauty, and veneration of the Blessed Virgin caused him to seek private funds for the erection of a statue.

On December 8, 1857, the statue was unveiled in the Piazza de Spagna. A long marble column rose from the center of the square. Atop the column stood a marble figure of the Virgin with outstretched arms, in the pose shown to Catherine Labouré. The next year, 1858, a beautiful lady appeared at Lourdes and told Bernadette: "I am the Immaculate Conception."

---

[8] Frances Thornton, *Cross Upon Cross* (New York: Benziger Brothers, 1955), 150–151.

· ·

CHAPTER 11

THE IMMACULATE AND FRANCE

The story is told of a French officer who toured the Papal Palace with his wife and two children shortly before Pius IX returned from exile. The officer's Protestant wife refused to attend Mass and resisted her husband's attempts to convert her. She became separated from the family during the tour and wandered into Pius IX's private chapel. The woman used the pope's kneeler to pray for God to protect her family.

Seized by a sudden fervor, she began consecrating her children to the Blessed Virgin. Light enveloped her. Above the altar she saw a luminous vision of Mary holding each of her children by the hand. Next to the altar stood a silver-haired man dressed in white. The woman pondered the vision but told no one what she had seen.

Days later the Protestant woman saw the silver-haired man again. It was Pope Pius IX entering Rome in solemn procession. As Pius blessed the cheering crown the woman again saw the Blessed Virgin above him. Once more she kept the vision to herself.

Later in the week she was presented to the pope along with wives of the other French officers. Pius caressed her children and gave them rosaries. Then he spoke to their mother, but she was unable to return the pope's kind remarks. Once more she saw the Blessed Virgin above the pope, and was rendered speechless.

After two sleepless nights, tear-filled nights wrestling with the Angel of the Lord, the Protestant woman gave in. She told her husband all she had seen and asked to be admitted into the Church. Her grateful husband placed his prized possession, the medal of St. Gregory given him by Pius IX, on the altar of God as an offering of thanksgiving for the Blessed Virgin's intercession with Pius IX, and with his wife.[1]

---

[1] Brennan, *Life of Pope Pius IX*, 270–272.

LTHOUGH neon was a century away, Rome glowed at night like a soul in a state of grace. Bells pealed, and cannons roared to celebrate Pius IX's honoring of the Blessed Virgin Mary. The joyous music resounding through the Eternal City was echoed in cities and villages around the world.

No country was more exuberant than France, where the propagation of the Miraculous Medal spread quickly throughout Europe. This gave popular impetus to the definition of Mary's Immaculate Conception. In recognition of this, and mindful of France's anti-Catholic republic,[2] Pius composed this prayer:

"O Mary! Conceived without sin, look down upon France, pray for France, save France! The greater her guilt, the more need of your intercession. Only a word to Jesus reposing in your arms, and France is saved. O Jesus! obedient to Mary, save France!"[3]

LOURDES

A short four years later, the Blessed Virgin appeared in 1858 at Lourdes, a small village in southwest France. During her eighteen visits to Lourdes, Mary did not weep as she had at La Salette. She even smiled when a teenaged peasant girl named Bernadette Soubirous responded to her appearance by kneeling and praying the Rosary.

During Mary's eighth appearance, it was fourteen-year-old Bernadette who wept. After repeatedly prostrating herself before her invisible visitor, Bernadette turned to the large crowd and, through her sobs, sounded the same warning Lúcia dos Santos would echo almost sixty years later: "Penance, Penance, Penance!"[4]

---

[2] After dragging their heels, the French government grudgingly allowed the publication in France of *Ineffabilis Deus,* the bull defining the dogma of Mary's Immaculate Conception.

[3] M. Aladel, C. M., *The Miraculous Medal, Its Origin, History, Circulation, Results,* trans. from the French (Preserving Christian Publications, Inc., 1999), 198.

[4] Rev. S. Pruvost, *The Wonders of Massabielle at Lourdes,* trans. Rev. Joseph

As with Lúcia, the Virgin also told Bernadette to "Pray
for sinners." When "the Lady" (as Bernadette called her)
appeared on March 25, the feast of the Annunciation, Bernadette repeatedly asked her name. In response:

> The lady assumed a serious aspect, and appeared
> to humble herself. She joined both hands and
> placed them upon her breast. She raised her eyes
> heavenward; then slowly separating her hands and
> leaning a trifle towards me, she uttered with a
> trembling voice these words: "I am the Immac-
> ulate Conception!" Immediately afterwards the
> Virgin disappeared.[5]

DAUGHTERS OF CHARITY

Young and illiterate Bernadette did not understand
the Lady's words. But her parish priest did. So did most
adult Catholics, who recognized Lourdes as heaven's seal of
approval on Pio Nono's definition of the Immaculate Conception. Also elated was Sister Catherine Labouré in Paris.
When hearing news of Lourdes, she exclaimed, "You see, it
is our own Blessed Mother, the Immaculate!"[6]

Catherine belonged to the Daughters of Charity,[7] an order
founded in the 1600s by St. Vincent de Paul and St. Louise
de Marillac. Monsieur Vincent (as he was commonly called)
never intended his Daughters to be nuns. Under the direction
of Vincent and Louise, a confraternity of wealthy Parisian
noblewomen was created to take in volunteers — mostly young
country girls recruited by Monsieur Vincent. The noble ladies
supervised the girls' spiritual and corporal works of charity

---

A. Fredette (Boston: The Lourdes Company, 1925) 46. Lúcia cried
"Penance!" after the Miracle of the Sun at Fatima, October 13, 1917.
[5] Ibid., p. 104.
[6] Joseph I. Dirvin, C. M., *Saint Catherine Laboure of the Miraculous
Medal* (reprint, Rockford, IL: TAN Books and Publishers, 1984), 179.
[7] Also known as the Sisters of Charity, and the Sisters of St. Vincent
de Paul. In France they were called the "Grey Sisters." In America,
there are other variations, including the "Grey Nuns," the "Black Cap
Sisters," and the "White Cap" or "Cornette" Sisters.

among the poor and the sick in Paris. The girls met weekly with Monsieur Vincent for encouragement and instruction.

Louise pressed Vincent for a more formal rule, which he eventually provided — sort of. Fearing too much structure would impede his Daughters' direct aid to the poor, Vincent's rule contained "no grate but the fear of God, and no veil but holy modesty."[8] Eventually, a formal rule was reluctantly accepted.

Some years later, Louise de Marillac prevailed upon Monsieur Vincent to formalize a vow she and the Daughters wished to make to Mary. Consequently, on December 8, 1658, the Order of the Daughters of Charity was consecrated to the Immaculate Virgin in a ceremony that stated, in part:

> Thou hast inspired us, Lord, to choose Thy Holy Mother as the unique Mother of our little Congregation... As we are the smallest and weakest, it is we who have need of Thy maternal succour... Suffer therefore that we may have recourse to Thee with trust, respect, humility and total submission...[9]

These virtues made many Daughters unflinching martyrs of the French Revolution. The order was still trying to build up its pre-Revolution numbers when Zoé Laboure joined them in 1830. Taking Catherine as her religious name, she was sent to the motherhouse in Paris.

She arrived at the same time that the incorrupt body of St. Vincent, carefully hidden from the hatred of the Revolution, was restored to the Vincentian Fathers of Paris.

THE MIRACULOUS MEDAL

The pomp and solemnity of the restoration ceremonies touched the heart of the young peasant girl. Catherine

---

[8] *The Catholic Encyclopedia* (Old Edition), s.v. "Sisters of Charity of St. Vincent de Paul."
[9] As quoted in *CRC*, September 2000, "Martyrdom of Saint Catherine Labouré," 25.

prayed to Monsieur Vincent for his order and for France, "ever the delight and the despair of the Church of Christ."[10]

With love and devotion, she then invoked her angel and the Blessed Virgin. It was eleven o'clock at night on July 18, 1830, the eve of the feast of St. Vincent de Paul, when Sister Catherine was awakened by a small boy[11] who said, "Come to the chapel, the Blessed Virgin awaits you."

She waited in the chapel until, with a rustle of silk, the Virgin appeared in the sanctuary and sat down. Sister Catherine threw herself at Mary's feet and clasped her hands together on the Virgin's knees.

"At this moment," Catherine recalled, "I felt the sweetest emotion of my life." The Virgin entrusted Catherine with a mission, warned her of trials to come, and with sadness said:

> My child, the times are very disastrous, great trials are about to come upon France, the throne will be overturned, the entire world will be in confusion by reason of miseries of every kind...
>
> Among the clergy in Paris there will be victims. Mgr. the Archbishop will die. My child, the cross will be despised, it will be trampled underfoot, our Lord's side will be opened anew, the streets will flow with blood, the entire world will be in tribulation.
>
> Catherine wondered when this would happen, and an "interior light distinctly indicated" the answer: forty years.[12]

In 1870 Mary's prophecy was fulfilled when Archbishop Darboy of Paris was murdered by Communists. Her other prophecy, the overthrow of the throne of Charles X, occurred ten days after her first appearance to Catherine.[13]

---

[10] Dirvin, *Saint Catherine Labouré of the Miraculous Medal*, 64.
[11] Later, Catherine expressed the conviction that it was really her guardian angel who appeared to her in the form of a boy.
[12] Aladel, The Miraculous Medal, 47–48.
[13] Known as the "Three Glorious Days," among radicals, mob members, and some historians. Charles was France's king of the Restoration.

The Immaculate had not come to Paris only to prophesy, however. Her real reason was revealed during her second visit to Catherine on the eve of the first Sunday of Advent, 1830.

Catherine was meditating in the chapel with other order members when she heard silk rustling, then saw the Blessed Virgin appear in the sanctuary.

"Her height was medium," Catherine said later, "and her countenance, indescribably beautiful. She was dressed in a robe the color of the dawn." Mary stood on a globe, her heel planted firmly on the head of a large serpent.[14] In her hands she held another, smaller globe. Her eyes "were raised to heaven, and her countenance beamed with light as She offered the globe to Our Lord."

"Suddenly her fingers were covered with rings and most beautiful, precious stones. Rays of dazzling light gleamed forth from them, and the whole of Her figure was enveloped in such radiance that her feet and robe were no longer visible . . . the Blessed Virgin fixed her eyes on me and a voice said in the depths of my heart: 'This globe which you see represents the whole world, especially France, and each person in particular.'"[15]

The Virgin told Catherine the dazzling light streaming from her hands was "the graces I shed upon those who ask me for them." "She made me understand," said Catherine, "how generous she is to all who implore her intercession . . . how many favors she grants to those who ask her for them with confidence, and the joy that she experienced in granting graces." Then Catherine saw an oval frame form around the Virgin, and the words: "*O Mary conceived without sin, pray for us who have recourse to Thee.*"

---

[14] Although the Immaculate appeared in front of all the Daughters, Catherine was the only one who saw her. Catherine "described the serpent to her director as 'green with yellow spots'—a rather fearsome serpent..." see Dirvin, Saint Catherine Labouré of the Miraculous Medal, 97.

[15] "In describing the brilliant rays that flashed from Mary's hands Catherine uses the word *rejaillissant*, thus suggesting a breathtaking picture of dazzling light 'bursting from all sides,' like a fountain." Ibid., 100.

Mary told Catherine: "Have a medal struck upon this model. All those who wear it, when it is blessed, will receive great graces, especially if they wear it round the neck. Those who repeat this prayer with devotion will be in a special manner under the protection of the Mother of God. Graces will be abundantly bestowed upon those who have confidence."[16]

Within two years, the Medal of the Immaculate Conception was made. France was in the grip of a fearsome cholera epidemic. The distribution of the medals "immediately effected such wonders that they soon merited the popular name of 'Miraculous Medals.'"[17] In addition to healing cholera victims, the Archbishop of Paris was a personal witness to the medal's miraculous conversion of a career criminal. The cures, conversions, and other prodigies continue to this day.

On the back of the medal, underneath the letter 'M' surmounted by a cross, are replicas of the Sacred Heart, encircled by thorns, and the Immaculate Heart, pierced by a sword. Devotion to the Holy Hearts is as old as the Church, but specific devotions to the Sacred Heart and the Immaculate Heart were formally established in France, during the "great age of souls"—that phenomenal explosion of mysticism, piety, and Catholic Action in seventeenth-century Counter-Reformation France that flowed from the Council of Trent.

COUNTER REFORMATION FRANCE

Francis de Sales, Monsieur Vincent, St. Jeanne de Chantal, the salon of Madame Barbe Acarie,[18] Baron de Renty and

---

[16] Catherine's account of the Virgin's second visit is from *Mary's Miraculous Medal* (Richmond, NH: The Slaves of the Immaculate Heart of Mary, 1999), 13–16.

[17] CRC, September 2000, 30.

[18] Also known as Blessed Marie of the Incarnation, "La Belle Acarie" was a housewife and an extraordinary mystic who helped bring the Carmelites to France and bore the stigmata.

the Company of the Blessed Sacrament, Pierre Bérulle and his French School of Theology, and prodigies like St. John Eudes and St. Louis de Montfort—these are only a scattering of the personalities of that remarkable period.[19]

The results were a reformed clergy and a more systematic study of devotion to the Holy Hearts. Père Eudes was instrumental in establishing official Church liturgies for the Sacred Heart and the Immaculate Heart. Heaven's response was the apparitions of the Sacred Heart to Margaret Mary in 1673, in Paray-le-Monial—only a few miles from where Catherine Labouré was born.

The devil's replies were, chronologically: Gallicanism, Jansenism, and the French Revolution. Each sought to destroy the fruits of France's Counter-Reformation. Yet just as the destructive fury of Calvinism helped prepare the ground for the great age of souls—by watering it with the blood of martyrs—so did the French Revolution precede another great mystical display by the Church's Eldest Daughter in the nineteenth century.

This later demonstration featured the Blessed Virgin Mary in person. She did not appear to the rulers of France, choosing instead to visit peasant folk like Mélanie and Maximin, Bernadette, Catherine Labouré, and others, such as Justine Bisqueyburu.

THE GREEN SCAPULAR

Justine was, like Catherine Labouré, a novice with the Daughters of Charity in Paris. In a series of apparitions in 1840,[20] Mary directed her to have made a small badge of green cloth, which on one side showed a representation of Mary very similar to the Immaculate Medal. The other side showed a heart pierced with a sword and "all ablaze with

---

[19] After writing eleven volumes on seventeenth-century France, the erudite Abbé Brémond declared this barely began to tell the story.
[20] The primary apparition concerning the Green Scapular happened September 8, 1840, in Blangy, France, where Justine had been sent to teach.

rays more dazzling than the sun and transparent as crystal."[21]

This Badge of the Immaculate Heart is better known today as the Green Scapular. It was made to convert the faithless and obtain for them a happy death. It could be worn, placed in clothing, or put in someone's room, as long as this was accompanied by the (preferably daily) prayer: "Immaculate Heart of Mary, pray for us now and at the hour of our death."

So Mary was at work in France for centuries before she joined forces with Pius IX. When the profound relationship between the Blessed Virgin and Blessed Pius IX reached its visible culmination in 1854, those with ears heard the angels sing.

---

[21] Don Sharkey, *The Woman Shall Conquer: The Story of the Blessed Virgin in the Modern World* (Milwaukee: The Bruce Publishing Company, 1952), 29.

CHAPTER 12

· ·

THE FATHERS RATISBONNE

HE confessor of Justine Bisqueyburu and Catherine Labouré was Father Aladel. It was his privilege — and burden — to announce the visions of his
two Daughters to his superiors and to obtain the necessary
permission for the Miraculous Medal and the Badge of the
Immaculate Heart (Green Scapular).

In addition to Father Aladel, Catherine and the other
Daughters had the services of the local pastor, Father Charles
du Friche des Gennettes. In 1832, Father des Gennettes was
transferred to Our Lady of Victories parish in Paris.

This church was built in 1629 by Louis XIII in thanksgiving to the Blessed Virgin for favors received. It was still recov-
ering from the French Revolution. Attendance was very low.
For years Father des Gennettes labored, in vain it seemed, to
increase the number of parishioners. On December 3, 1836,
while saying Mass in the virtually empty church, Father was

> Seized by a frightful distraction, the conviction
> that he must resign. He could scarcely keep his
> mind on the Mass. When he reached the Canon,
> he cried out in distress. At that moment, he heard
> a calm, distinct voice say very solemnly: "Conse-
> crate your parish to the Most Holy and Immacu-
> late Heart of Mary."[1]

Father resolved to do so and told the few parishioners
about his intentions. On the night in question Father entered
Our Lady of Victories to find it full. More than 400 people
attended — not just that night but regularly thereafter. Within
two years, Pope Gregory XVI elevated Father des Gennettes'

---

[1] Sharkey, *The Woman Shall Conquer: The Story of the Blessed Virgin in the Modern World*, 25–26.

growing confraternity to the "Archconfraternity of the Holy
and Immaculate Heart of Mary for the Conversion of Sinners."[2]

FATHER THEODORE RATISBONNE

The following year, 1839, Our Lady of Victories parish was
swarmed by sinners and converts. The Archconfraternity grew
so large Father des Gennettes took on an assistant: Father
Theodore Ratisbonne, a Jewish convert from Strasbourg.[3]

Father Ratisbonne's salary consisted of sharing frugal
meals with Father des Gennettes. He appeared well satisfied
with this meager fare, calling his new position "a privilege
I owe to Mary." His duties included voluminous correspondence and face-to-face contacts with people from all over
the world expressing interest in the now flourishing parish
of Our Lady of Victories. "The Sacristy of *Notre-Dame des
Victoires* is Rome in miniature," Father Ratisbonne told a
friend, "a center of life and grace."[4]

Born to a wealthy Jewish family connected to the Rothschilds, Theodore Ratisbonne was a thoughtful, reflective,
and patient man. His conversion to Catholicism was years in
coming, but once it began Theodore would not be denied.
He was baptized in 1827 on September 12, the feast of the
Holy Name of Mary. Three years later he was ordained a
priest. It was the last straw for his family.

> "I remember one day," Father Theodore recalled,
> "my old uncle saying in a moment of despair that
> he would rather see me torn in a thousand pieces

---

[2] The worldwide devotion to Our Lady of Victories that grew out of
these events is primarily a devotion to the Immaculate Heart. Father
des Genettes also felt an alliance with the visions of Catherine Labouré.
Consequently, Archconfraternity members are enjoined to wear a Miraculous Medal and to recite the prayer to the Immaculate Conception. See
M. Aladel, *The Miraculous Medal: Its Origin, History, Circulation, Results*, 43.
[3] Strasbourg was in Alsace, which at that time was part of France.
[4] Both quotations in this paragraph are from *A Nineteenth Century
Miracle: The Brothers Ratisbonne and the Congregation of Notre-Dame de
Sion*, trans. L. M. Leggatt (London: Burns Oates & Washbourne, 1922),
64, 67, respectively.

than wearing a cassock. 'You would gain nothing by that,' I answered quietly, 'for if I were torn to pieces each separate part of my body would become a priest, and instead of one cassock you would have a thousand."[5]

Praying at his father's deathbed he was set upon by other Jewish family members. Later he said:

It was an awful moment! I fell on my knees beside the bed and defended myself, crying out with my whole strength, "Jesus, save me!" And this cry, bursting from my breaking heart, gave the last shock to my father on his deathbed. May that Name, the last word he heard on leaving this world, have been his first on entering Eternity![6]

Shortly before coming to Our Lady of Victories, Father Ratisbonne suffered another painful family encounter. His young nephew was seriously ill. Theodore resolved to speak to his brother, the boy's father, about baptism. Before he could do so, another brother, Alphonse, interfered, and in a "paroxysm of rage," drove Father Ratisbonne away from the dying child.[7] Father Theodore left Strasbourg for Paris and Our Lady of Victories, vowing that "he would not cease to pray for the conversion of his brothers and sisters."[8]

ALPHONSE RATISBONNE

Alphonse was not impressed by his brother's prayers. He admittedly "cherished a bitter hatred against priests, churches, and convents, and especially against the Jesuits, whose very name goaded me to frenzy."[9] Since he was not a practicing Jew and said he "believed in nothing," his vehemence was

---

[5] Ibid., 45.
[6] Ibid., 49.
[7] Ibid., 65.
[8] *The Conversion of Ratisbonne, Narratives of Alphonse Ratisbonne and Baron Theodore de Bussières* (Fort Collins, CO: Roman Catholic Books, 2000), 54.
[9] Ibid., 53.

curious.

Little else seemed to bother Alphonse. He was an intelligent young man in a position to choose any lucrative career he wished, thanks in part to Baron Rothschild, "whose family lavished on me every kind of attention."[10] Moreover, he was engaged to a beautiful young woman whom he was also in love with. Ironically, it was Rothschild who urged Alphonse to travel to Rome to mark time until his fiancée was old enough to marry.

Alphonse did take a voyage, but he was determined *not* to go to Rome. Through an unforeseen series of accidents, however, he ended up in Rome on January 6, 1842 — the feast of Epiphany and the anniversary of his brother Theodore's first Mass. Once in Rome, other unforeseen events foiled Alphonse's plans to leave. His hatred toward Catholicism grew — if that were possible — upon seeing the Roman ghetto.

He visited Baron Theodore de Bussières, an acquaintance from Alsace who was living in Rome. Bussières bore the brunt of a lengthy, ill-tempered tirade against Catholicism by his fellow Alsatian. When Alphonse paused for breath Bussierès, a Catholic convert, asked him to wear a Miraculous Medal.

Ratisbonne backed away, but Bussières pressed him: "As you look at things, this should be an indifferent matter in your eyes, while it will give me a great deal of pleasure." Ratisbonne was caught, and he knew it. He donned the medal, then burst out in sarcastic laughter: "Ah! Ha! I am now become Catholic, Apostolic, and Roman!"[11]

As part of the bargain, Ratisbonne also agreed to pray the *Memorare*. As he again prepared to leave Rome, he was surprised to find himself silently repeating the *Memorare*. He was even more surprised when he canceled his plan to leave. He still thought Catholic devotion "hopelessly, grotesquely mad,"[12] but on January 20, 1842, he somehow found himself

---

[10] Ibid., 58.
[11] "It was the devil who prophesied through my mouth," Ratisbonne said later. See *Mary's Miraculous Medal*, 26.
[12] *The Conversion of Ratisbonne*, 67.

still in Rome and entering the small, poor church of *San't Andrea delle Fratte.*

CONVERSION

> "I was looking around mechanically, without any definite thought or purpose," he said later. "I remember only a black dog, which bounded and jumped before me as I moved about. Suddenly the dog disappeared. The whole church disappeared; I saw nothing further. Or rather, O my God, I saw only one object!" [13]

Baron de Bussières had left Ratisbonne alone for perhaps fifteen minutes. He returned to find the irreligious Jew kneeling rapt in prayer before the Chapel of the Archangels Michael and Raphael. After repeatedly shaking him, Alphonse finally looked up and Bussières saw tears streaming down his face.

Alphonse pulled out his Miraculous Medal, and kissing it fervently declared: "I have seen her, I have seen her!" Bussières half-carried Alphonse out of the church, asking what had happened. Ratisbonne shook his head and for the very first time asked to see a priest. "What I saw," he told Bussières, "I can only speak of on my knees." [14]

He saw what Catherine saw; what Bernadette saw; what Mélanie and Maximin saw; what perhaps Blessed Pius IX saw when formally declaring the dogma of the Immaculate Conception: someone you instinctively kneel before, someone who melts your heart and evokes unbidden tears of joy, love, and longing. Only when he was finally before a priest would Alphonse tell of a light he saw coming from one of the chapels in the darkened church:

> In the midst of this radiance I saw, standing at the Altar, lofty, clothed with splendor, full of majesty

---

[13] Ibid., 70.
[14] *A Nineteenth Century Miracle*, 78.

and sweetness, the Virgin Mary, just as she is rep-
resented on my Medal. An irresistible force drew
me towards her. She made a sign with her hand
for me to kneel down; she spoke not a word but
I understood all. [15]

The medal depicted rays of light Catherine saw streaming
from the hands of the Immaculate. Alphonse Ratisbonne
saw it too. [16] He could not behold her face, for she was too
beautiful. But her hands were at eye level for someone on
his knees, and of the hands of Mary, Ratisbonne would later
say they "expressed all the secrets of divine pity."

> I could not express (he said) what I saw of mercy
> and liberality in Mary's hands. It was not only an
> effulgence of light; it was not rays I distinguished.
> Words are inadequate to depict the ineffable gifts
> filling our Mother's hands and descending from
> them, the bounty, mercy, tenderness, the celes-
> tial sweetness and riches, flowing in torrents and
> inundating the souls She protects. [17]

Not a word did she speak, but after kneeling before the
Queen of Heaven Alphonse said he "knew all." [18] He knew
to whom he owed his conversion: "The Blessed Virgin, who
obtained it from God, and to the prayers of my brother, who
is one of the Directors of the Archconfraternity of *Notre-
Dame des Victoires*." [19]

While Alphonse surely remembered Theodore's vow to
pray for him, he was probably unaware that Theodore had
also written a book on St. Bernard of Clairvaux, the author of
the *Memorare* prayer Alphonse was unable to stop repeating.

As will be seen, the conversion of Alphonse Ratisbonne
became worldwide news.

---

[15] Ibid., p. 78.
[16] Later Lúcia, Francisco, and Jacinta would see the same rays of light
at Fatima.
[17] *Mary's Miraculous Medal*, 31.
[18] Dirvin, *Saint Catherine Labouré of the Miraculous Medal*, 169.
[19] Ibid.

CHAPTER 13

WHAT IT ALL MEANS

MARIE ALPHONSE RATISBONNE

Theodore Ratisbonne's conversion had been the product of years of patient, deliberate study. His brother Alphonse's conversion took roughly fifteen minutes, but now even this seemed an unbearably long time to have met the Immaculate and still be outside the Church.

When it was suggested he defer baptism until the passion of the moment subsided, Alphonse was beside himself: "*What?* The Jews were baptized as soon as they had heard the Apostles, and you want to keep me waiting when I have heard the Queen of Apostles?"[1]

Eleven days later, he received the sacraments. Clad in a long white robe, a rosary clasped tightly in his hand, he repeatedly gazed at the image on his medal, as if reliving those sublime moments when the grace of heaven flowed through the hands of Mary and into his very being.

After the prayers of exorcism, he was asked what his new name was. "Marie," he blurted out, as if eager for the chance to say her name aloud. After his baptism he received the sacrament of confirmation. Then, appearing profoundly recollected, Marie Alphonse Ratisbonne attended his first Mass:

> When the solemn moment was reached and the Cardinal, his hand trembling with emotion, laid the Sacred Host on the tongue of the neophyte, Ratisbonne, hitherto so calm and self-controlled in all his fervour, burst into sobs...
>
> At last, the Te Deum rang out in a torrent of sound from the hearts of all present; it was no

---

[1] *A Nineteenth Century Miracle,* 79.

mere solemn rhythmic chant, but the loud accla-
mation of a multitude swept by the enthusiasm
of their faith.[2]

News of the miracle went worldwide. Father Theodore
received a letter from Bussières and Marie Alphonse on —
fittingly enough — the feast of the Purification. His joy can
perhaps be imagined. Afterward, he tried to give a sermon
"but in spite of all my efforts to keep calm I broke down
completely and my tears flowed upon the Altar." He reassured an anxious audience as to his health, then told them
his great good news:

> When the name I was trying not to reveal came
> from my heart in spite of myself, a mighty thrill
> passed over the whole assembly and with one
> voice all the orphan girls began to chant the
> *Magnificat* . . . I nearly fainted several times before
> I could finish my Mass, but I hope God forgave
> my weakness.[3]

That evening, Our Lady of Victories parish was standing
room only. Father des Gennettes remembered:

> When Father Ratisbonne, after describing the cir-
> cumstances of this astounding conversion, said
> "This convert is my brother. . ." a loud exclama-
> tion came from the huge congregation, as if an
> electric shock had passed through them all. Many
> tears of joy were shed. For a year past, they had all
> been praying fervently for the Ratisbonne family,
> and Father Theodore had more than once asked
> the Archconfraternity for prayers for his brother
> Alphonse. It is impossible to describe the enthusi-
> asm of the multitude as they sang the *Magnificat*,
> and it soon spread to all the other Catholics in
> the town.[4]

---

[2] Ibid., 82–83.
[3] Ibid., 84–85.
[4] *A Nineteenth Century Miracle*, 85.

Two months later, Marie Alphonse came to Paris to visit Father Theodore and his miraculous church. It was the first time they had seen each other since a raging Alphonse drove Theodore away from their sick nephew.

Now, Marie Alphonse Ratisbonne was transfigured. When he tried to describe his encounter with the Immaculate, however, words surrendered to sobs: "The two brothers embraced with tears and thanksgivings to God, and the subject was never mentioned again between them."[5]

Never had Our Lady of Victories parish seemed more aptly named.

WHAT IT ALL MEANS

Later that same remarkable year, a French religious came across a chest full of old books and papers. In it, he found a manuscript by Louis-Marie Grignion de Montfort that had been hidden away during the Revolution.

Although the doctrine of St. Louis de Montfort was classic French School and could have been written by any of Louis' mentors,[6] what clinched the question of authorship of *True Devotion to Mary* was the unmistakable stamp of Louis' personal piety and zeal, which in matters regarding Mary, burned white hot. The works of Louis were put back in circulation.

So what does any of this have to do with Blessed Pius IX? Well, at the beginning of this book I said I wanted to put Pius' words and deeds in their proper historical context. What you are reading is that context.

Giovanni Maria Mastai-Ferretti grew up and became pope in a century that featured both the sinister machinations of Freemasonry and the dramatic emergence of the Immaculate Virgin Mary as the deadly opponent of Lucifer—just as St. Louis de Montfort had predicted a century before his prophecy was rediscovered.[7]

---

[5] Ibid., 86.
[6] He was the last disciple of the original French School.
[7] St. Louis De Montfort, *True Devotion to Mary* (Rockford: IL: TAN Books and Publishers, 1985), 25–36.

The Immaculate appeared most often in France — admonishing, warning, healing, curing, converting, offering mercy and grace, and leaving the sweet fragrance of miracles in her wake. The French people loved her; their leaders did not. France would pay a dear price for the corruption of its rulers.

One of many beneficiaries of the Immaculate was Blessed Pius IX, whom she cured of epilepsy. There is much about the relationship between the Immaculate and Blessed Pius IX that remains veiled, but we know enough to conclude with confidence that he was a truly Marian pope. He himself has said so.

When he assumed the Chair of Peter, Pius proclaimed: "Nothing have we had more at heart — a heart which from our tenderest years has overflowed with devoted veneration and love for the most Blessed Virgin — than to show her prerogatives in resplendent light."[8]

His deeds followed his words. He sought to glorify Mary by proclaiming the truth of her Immaculate Conception, and he honored her by rescuing from the clutches of the Revolution every soul he could for her Son, no matter the cost in human terms.

Like the soul of Edgardo Levi Mortara, a young Jewish boy whose conversion was every bit as real, permanent, and remarkable as the conversion of Alphonse Ratisbonne. Equally remarkable is Blessed Pius IX's steadfast protection of the spiritual welfare of this one solitary lost sheep. He didn't have to do it, but he did. Some say Pius' stalwart defense of young Mortara cost the last Pope-King his kingdom.

---

[8] Pius IX, *Ineffabilis Deus: Apostolic Constitution Defining the Dogma of the Immaculate Conception* (1854; reprint, Boston: St. Paul Books and Media), 18–19.

CHAPTER 14

. . . .

"THE MORTARA AFFAIR"

THE conversion of Alphonse Ratisbonne was an immediate infusion of divine truth as dramatic and permanent as the lightning flash from heaven that knocked Saul of Tarsus off his mule.

The intense interest in the event prompted a Church investigation, which "affirmed the reality and truth of the miracle wrought by God, at the intercession of the Blessed Virgin Mary, in the instantaneous and perfect conversion from Judaism of Alphonse Ratisbonne."[1]

At first the recipient of the perfect conversion was overwhelmed. "My earnest wish," Marie Alphonse Ratisbonne confessed, "was to bury myself in a Trappist monastery" to "find refuge from a world which no longer understood me. I confess I thought my family and friends would consider me insane, that they would turn me to ridicule."[2] One may smile at Ratisbonne's reluctance to receive the same scorn and incredulity he once delighted in heaping on Catholics, but there is no denying he had much to lose by converting — and in short order he lost it all. His lucrative banking career disappeared, he was disinherited by his uncle, his engagement was broken, and he was disowned by his family.

How did Ratisbonne react to these reversals of fortune? He murmured not a word. Instead, he entered the Society of Jesus,[3] became a priest, and with his brother Theodore, founded *Notre-Dame de Sion* — Our Lady of Zion — a community dedicated to the conversion of Jews.

---

[1] The text of the Decree Verifying and Accrediting the Miracle, as presented in *The Conversion of Ratisbonne*, 84.
[2] Ibid., 72.
[3] Prior to his conversion, the mere mention of the word "Jesuit" could incite Alphonse Ratisbonne to a frenzy.

In 1847, Pius IX addressed an apostolic brief to the Ratisbonne brothers, which "granted very precious indulgences
to the actual and future members of the devout community."[4] Pius also attached generous indulgences to the *Memorare* prayer.[5]

In 1855, Pius allowed Marie Alphonse to leave the Jesuits
to bring the Daughters of Zion to Jerusalem. When the nuns
came to Rome to have their constitutions approved, Pius
was delighted. "The Daughters of Father Ratisbonne!" he
exclaimed upon seeing them. "Those dear Ratisbonnes," he
said, "tell them I bless them with all my heart!"[6]

The double blessing by the Immaculate and Pio Nono
upon their efforts bore good fruit: of the many Jews the
Ratisbonnes converted during their lives as priests, twenty-
eight were members of their own family.[7]

HOW THINGS WERE

Many in the Church hoped the conversion of Ratisbonne
was the beginning of the mass conversion of the Jewish
race that some Church Fathers thought would herald the
Second Coming.

But the extraordinary conversions of the Ratisbonne
brothers stood in stark contrast to the activities of their
fellow Jews — like Karl Marx. Moreover, Jewish historian
Cecil Roth asserts:

> In the various phases of the *Risorgimento* in Italy,
> the Jews were playing an exceptionally important
> part. The Roman Republic under Mazzini, the
> Venetian Republic under Manin (himself of Jew-
> ish descent), the various enterprises of Garibaldi,
> owed more proportionately to the Jews than to
> any other section of the Italian people. In 1848,

---

[4] *A Nineteenth Century Miracle*, 116.
[5] Including a plenary indulgence once a month, under the usual
conditions.
[6] *A Nineteenth Century Miracle*, 263.
[7] *Mary's Miraculous Medal*, 33.

the liberal government of the Kingdom of Sardinia (Piedmont), which was assuming the lead in the struggle for the unity of Italy, enfranchised its Jewish subjects.[8]

Masonic revolutions tended to include some form of Jewish emancipation, either by direct law or indirectly by the suppression of the Church and the secularization of government and culture. While few Jews mourned the suppression of the Church, not all wished to be emancipated. Many remained in the ghetto after the Gentiles razed the walls, even in lands ruled by the pope — a fact remarked upon by Pius IX to Father Theodore Ratisbonne:

> At his [Ratisbonne's] first audience, Pius IX had spoken at length of all the efforts he intended making to break down the existing barriers between the Jews of the Papal States and the rest of the Christian population. "But," the Pontiff went on to say, "the very people who begged so long for this freedom have refused to profit by it now it is offered them."[9]

One might assume any Jew unfortunate enough to be born into that bastion of bigotry, malice, and superstition known as the Papal States would have seized the first opportunity to flee to liberal Piedmont. No doubt some did, but many Jews — about fifteen thousand — chose to stay in the Papal States. Almost a thousand lived in Bologna, the second-largest city (after Rome) in the States, and the one with the most synagogues (eleven).[10]

Bologna's distance from Rome was more than geographic. It was a university city whose business climate attracted merchants like Salomone (Momolo) Mortara, who moved

---

[8] Cecil Roth, *A History of the Jews: From Earliest Times Through the Six-Day War,* rev. ed. (New York: Schocken Books, 1970), 331–332.
[9] *A Nineteenth Century Miracle,* 136.
[10] David I. Kertzer, *The Kidnapping of Edgardo Mortara* (New York: Alfred A. Knopf, 1997), 13.

his family to Bologna in 1850.[11] The following year, on August 27, 1851, his wife Marianna, gave birth to a son, Edgardo. Momolo hired a servant to help Marianna: Anna Morisi, a Catholic girl from San Giovanni, a small town outside Bologna.

THE BAPTISM OF EDGARDO MORTARA

It was illegal for a Catholic like Anna to be a servant for the Jewish Mortaras. This was forbidden not just in the Papal States but by canon law. Exactly one century before Edgardo Mortara was born, Pope Benedict XIV issued the encyclical *A Quo Primum* on relations between Christians and Jews. In decidedly unecumenical language Benedict declared to the Polish hierarchy:

> We follow the line of conduct adopted by Our Venerable Predecessors, the Roman Pontiffs. Alexander III (1159–1181) forbade Christians, under severe penalties, to enter the service of Jews for any lengthy period or to become domestic servants in their households. "They ought not," he wrote, "to serve Jews for pay in permanent fashion. Our ways of life and those of Jews are utterly different, and Jews will easily pervert the souls of simple folk to their superstition and unbelief, if such folk are living in continual and intimate converse with them."[12]

The reason Benedict wrote the Polish hierarchy, of course, was because laws regulating relations between Christians and Jews were *not* being observed. In the next century the same non-observance of the law occurred in the Papal

---

[11] Interestingly, the Mortaras moved to Bologna *after* the Austrians had driven off the revolutionary government and helped restore the papal government. It almost seemed the Mortaras preferred papal rule to Masonic rule.

[12] Benedict went on to quote Innocent III, Innocent IV, Nicholas IV, Paul IV, St. Pius V, Gregory XIII and Clement VIII to the same effect. See https://www.jewishvirtuallibrary.org/pope-benedict-xiv-on-jews.

States. The ban against Jews hiring Catholic servants was on the books but rarely enforced. The most common illegal arrangement was for Jewish families to hire young girls like Anna Morisi to work for the Mortaras on the Jewish Sabbath. In return, Anna earned money for a marriage dowry.

When Edgardo was a year old he contracted neuritis, a condition his doctor described as "most serious." Anna remembered his parents "sad and crying, at a little table next to Edgardo's crib, reading from a book in Hebrew that the Jews read when one of them is about to die."[13]

While on a shopping errand, Anna told the grocer about the dying Jewish baby. The grocer told her to baptize the baby and showed her how. Anna later testified:

> When I got back to the house, I saw that the parents were watching over their sick son, so I had to wait for about an hour. They finally left the living room and went to their bedroom. I quickly drew a little water from the well, went over to the boy's crib and repeated the words that I'd been taught, with the fixed idea of sending a soul to heaven. I put the fingers of my right hand in the glass of water, sprinkled a few drops on the boy's head, and in a moment it was all done, without anyone noticing.[14]

To everyone's surprise, shortly after being baptized Edgardo recovered completely. Several years later another Mortara infant became deathly ill. A neighbor servant girl told Anna to baptize the baby. "Not me," Anna replied, "I already baptized one of them, and I wouldn't want him to live like the other one did." Two days later the Mortara baby, Aristide, died unbaptized.

Anna stopped working for the Mortaras, but her admission was repeated to Father Feletti, the inquisitor. He

---

[13] From her testimony in 1859 to the Bologna magistrate, as quoted in Kertzer, *The Kidnapping of Edgardo Mortara*, 206.
[14] Ibid.

summoned Anna, and she admitted to secretly baptizing
Edgardo Mortara. Although this was done in secrecy, there
was no sinister intent involved. In fact, Anna believed she
had performed a work of mercy that allowed the small
baby to reach heaven. One may disagree with what she
did, but it is important to remember: these were the
beliefs of the time. Anna was trying to do a good deed.

The usual procedure in these cases — they happened a
lot — was to remove the baptized child for its own spiritual welfare, but a cautious Feletti first consulted the Holy
Office in Rome.

Although Pius IX was titular head of the Holy Office,[15]
there is no evidence he took part in or even knew about
these routine proceedings. Feletti was instructed to proceed. On Friday, June 25, 1858, six-year-old Edgardo was
removed from his home and taken to Rome to be edu-
cated as the Christian his baptism had made him.

This became known as the "Mortara Affair," which
is also the subject of a recent motion picture produced
by Steven Spielberg. At the time of Pius IX's beatification (2000) it was erroneously called a "kidnapping" after
David Kertzer's book *The Kidnapping of Edgardo Mortara*.[16]
This is misleading because a kidnapping is illegal. Whatever one may conclude about the Mortara case it is simply
a fact that, according to the laws of the time, Edgardo
Mortara was *not* illegally removed from his home.

The legality of little Edgardo's removal was small
comfort to his parents, who were devastated — but not

---

[15] Now it is the Dicastery for the Doctrine of the Faith.
[16] His fourth book. David I. Kertzer is a professor of anthropology and
history at Brown University and a scholar of nineteenth-century Italian
history. He dedicated his book to the memory of his father, Morris
Kertzer, a Jewish chaplain who once conducted a Sabbath ceremony
with Chief Rabbi Israel Zolli in the synagogue in Rome. When Zolli
converted to Catholicism, "the embarrassment of Italy's Jews could
scarcely have been greater, and denunciations of his (Zolli's) character,
his past, and even his sanity thundered from Jewish leaders far and
wide." According to Kertzer, "My father wrote in his defense." (304).

paralyzed. Momolo began working through Church chan-
nels to bring their plight to Pius IX in the belief that if the
Holy Father really knew what had happened, he would
return Edgardo to them.

No one knew at the time that little Edgardo's removal
from his home would become a worldwide controversy.

CHAPTER 15

AN INTERNATIONAL AFFAIR

I T was not the Mortara family but enemies of the Church who turned the Mortara Affair into an international controversy. Before getting into all that, however, it should be noted the Mortara's unhappiness was not due to ignorance of the law.

They knew it was illegal to have a Christian servant, and they knew that if a servant baptized one of their children, that child became a Christian, and the Church would not allow a Christian to be raised by Jews.

The Church teaches that baptism leaves an indelible mark on the soul that cannot be expunged for the sake of convenience or even family. Momolo and Marianna Mortara had personally witnessed other Jewish families who lost children secretly baptized by Catholic servants. According to Kertzer:

> The taking of Jewish children was a common occurrence in nineteenth-century Italy. So frequent had such cases become that in October 1851, a few weeks after Edgardo's birth, the leaders of the Jewish communities drew up a joint petition about "an extremely grave evil." We speak of the horrible danger that we face even today of, from one moment to the next, finding ourselves bereft of our offspring due to clandestine baptism.[1]

The simplest remedy was to obey the law and not hire Catholic servants. It seems surprising that Jewish parents not only broke the law but exposed their children to the "extremely grave evil" of sanctifying grace as well. "Although Jewish men and women spoke endlessly of the danger they

---

[1] Kertzer, *The Kidnapping of Edgardo Mortara*, 34.

faced," remarks Kertzer, "there is little evidence that they ever of their own accord sought to do without their Catholic servants." [2]

AN INTERNATIONAL AFFAIR

The Mortara case would have had little significance outside Italy except for two reasons. The first was the Church's enemies, particularly Piedmont's Prime Minister, Count Camillo de Cavour. [3] David Kertzer explains the second reason:

> The development of a relatively free press, intended for a mass audience, had by 1858 changed the dynamics of power in much of Western Europe. One part of this movement was the founding of Jewish newspapers.
>
> If the Mortara case became an international cause célèbre, it was in no small part due to the newly acquired ability of the Jews to make their grievances known publicly and to communicate and organize rapidly across national boundaries. The emancipated Jews profited not only from their newfound freedom of expression and freedom of the press, but from their increased political influence. [4]

In America "a stream of declamation and indignation poured forth from pulpit and press," particularly the Jewish press, where "no issue of the Jewish periodicals was published, for months on end, without some article, editorial, or report on the Mortara case." [5] The agitation on both sides of the Atlantic sought to persuade governments to intervene

---

[2] Ibid., 38. Servants did work Jews were not allowed to do on the Sabbath, such as gathering wood and making fires.
[3] Cavour coveted papal territory and had a powerful ally in French Emperor Napoleon III. England was sympathetic to Cavour's efforts to "unify" the Italian peninsula.
[4] Ibid., 43.
[5] Bertram Korn, *American Reaction to the Mortara Case, 1858–1859* (Cincinnati: American Jewish Archives, 1957), 72–73.

and force the Church to return Edgardo Mortara. As one American Rabbi put it:

> When Rome officially declares civil and religious liberty to be a damnable acquisition of our advanced age then it throws the gauntlet in the face of every dissenting Government, and no country is more insulted than this one, which considers civil and religious liberty the most precious jewel in the republican diadem of America.[6]

American Protestants joined the protest, causing some American Catholics to observe that while Jews and Protestants were rabidly indignant about the removal of one boy from his family, they seemed indifferent to the far more frequent separation of children from their parents in American slave trading, or the New York practice of picking up Catholic children for vagrancy and depositing them in Protestant institutions that barred priests from entering.[7]

For American Catholics, the "precious jewels" of civil and religious liberty appeared more rhetorical than real. Convert Orestes Brownson went further, saying the Jews deserved to be discriminated against due to their carrying on about the Mortara case. Another American Catholic declared:

> I am no enemy of the Jews. I do not wish to see them oppressed or persecuted. But when I see them displaying so much zeal in behalf of religious toleration, I cannot but regret that such liberal feelings did not actuate their co-religionists in the days of Jesus of Nazareth, the proto-martyr Stephen, and Saul of Tarsus.[8]

---

[6] Ibid., 74.

[7] Ibid., 150.

[8] Ibid., 146-7. Korn concludes, sourly, that American Catholics "refused to admit the superiority of the American tradition of the separation of church and state to the system of the Papal States" (155).

Despite the furor, the American government rejected Jewish and Protestant pressure for government intervention. On this point Kertzer notes:

> How could he [American President Buchanan] rail against a government that allowed a child to be forcibly separated from his parents when the same thing happened all the time in the slaveholding portions of his own country?[9]

Although European governments also refused to intervene, the line of claimants seeking to destroy the temporal authority of the pope grew.

THE PAPAL STATES

What exactly were the Papal States? Over the centuries the Church accumulated territories around Rome known as the Patrimony of St. Peter (later, Lazio). Additional territory in central Italy was also acquired. As the popes' influence grew, Italians relied on them for protection from barbarian invasions.

The Papal States were created in the 750s after Frankish King Pepin III answered the call of Pope Stephen II to protect the Italian peninsula from the Lombards. A portion of central Italy was formally recognized as the Republic of St. Peter. Later, it was called the Papal States.[10]

Over time, the wisdom of popes having their own territory was recognized. It protected the Church from political considerations influencing religious decisions.

By the 1800s the clamor over the Papal States was not new. Napoleon had seized them once. The later Mortara case only magnified indignation among the usual suspects, who were happy for the opportunity. But what was all the fuss about?

---

[9] Kertzer, *The Kidnapping of Edgardo Mortara*, 127.
[10] "Papal States," *Encyclopædia Britannica*, https://www.britannica.com/place/Papal-States.

CHAPTER 16

ABOUT THE PAPAL STATES

On April 12, 1855, the anniversary of Pope Pius IX's return to Rome from his exile in Gaeta, the Holy Father was invited to examine some newly discovered catacombs near the Church of St. Agnes. Escorted by several cardinals and bishops, Pius visited the site, which contained the bodies of Pope Alexander I and Saints Eventius and Theodulus.

Afterward the group ate lunch at the convent. The Pope was in his usual fine humor, and his group grew larger. Eventually eighty students were invited into the already crowded room by Pius, who was seated in a large, canopied armchair. Suddenly there was a loud snap, followed by a deafening crash. The timbers supporting the floor gave way, and the entire floor collapsed down into the room below. Giving an involuntary cry to the Blessed Virgin, Pius IX disappeared.

Rescuers frantically pushed away large beams and stones. Eventually, Pius was found — unharmed and (remarkably) unmarked — still seated in his chair. Others appeared so seriously injured that the dust-covered pope was asked to administer last rites. Pius said this would not be necessary, because, due to the intervention of the Blessed Virgin, no one would perish.

Then Pius turned to an American bishop creating clouds of dust by vigorously whacking the dirt off the pope's back. Pius asked the bishop to stop, noting that his behavior was "making our feast a veritable Ash Wednesday."

Afterward, Pius IX prayed a Mass in thanksgiving that no lives were lost. He was convinced this grace was due to the intercession of the Blessed Virgin. News of the incident at St. Agnes traveled around the world, generating much discussion. [1]

---

[1] https://zadokromanus.blogspot.com/2008/01/miracle-of-bl-piux-ix-at-st-agnes.html. This site contains the entire *NY Times* article on the incident. "Miracle of Bl. Pius IX at St. Agnes," *Zadok Romanus* (blog), January 2008.

REPORT ON THE PAPAL STATES

Public opinion had been shaped to regard the Papal States as a backward and impoverished land badly run by an oppressive and corrupt clerical government. Like any man-made government, the management of the Papal States was far from perfect. Yet were things so awful as to justify the insistent demands for "reform in the Papal States"? Or to seize the States from the Church to save its oppressed citizenry from deranged clerics?

The French ambassador to Rome, Count Alphonse de Rayneval, investigated the Papal States in 1856. His employer, Napoleon III, had an interest in documenting the claims he, Cavour, and Lord Palmerston were making about the wretchedness of life in the Papal States.

Rayneval took his assignment seriously. He conducted an exhaustive study of virtually all aspects of Church government in the Papal States and the condition of its citizens. The main criticism Rayneval had of governance in the States was the "partial occupation of its territory by foreign (Austrian) troops." Rayneval elaborated:

> Every independent state is expected to suffice for itself, and to be able to maintain its internal security by its own forces. The Court of Rome is reproached with falling short of this reasonable expectation.[2]

After noting the considerable unrest in the Papal States requiring better internal security, Rayneval traced the cause of the discontent: revolutionary agitation. The reason for the agitation, Rayneval believed, was the desire to make Italy a great world power:

> But how to create a powerful Italy so long as the peninsula is divided into two parts by a state neutral from the necessity of its nature and isolated from all European conflicts? How play a great

---

[2] O'Clery, *The Making of Italy*, 22.

part when the center of Italy is in possession of
a sovereign who doesn't wear a sword?[3]

After citing the presence in the States of the political
parties of Carbonari and the Mazzinians (*Young Italy*), Rayneval noted:

> The universal republic, the unity of Italy, consti-
> tutional government, war against Austria, is their
> programme. They say they are a numerous body
> and are ready to act, but they never keep their
> word...their watchword for the present is quiet
> and inaction, until the return of their chiefs by
> means of an amnesty, and the departure of the
> foreign troops give them an opportunity for act-
> ing with a chance of success.[4]

Rayneval then addressed the claim that thousands of
priests ran the States. He displayed a table proving most
positions in the papal government were staffed by laypeople.
The total number of priests holding government positions
throughout all the States was roughly one hundred.

Rayneval noted Pius IX emphasized that every position
in the papal government was open to laypeople, then asked:

> Is it possible to believe that the happiness and
> repose of the population are powerfully affected
> by the presence of such a small number of per-
> sons who have for the most part nothing of the
> ecclesiastical but the dress?[5]

He consulted with French legal scholars regarding the
laws of the Papal States and revealed their conclusion: the
laws "are above criticism...a model document."

As to the charge that pontifical governments did nothing for their citizens, Rayneval noted the pontifical government made "incessant efforts" to "ameliorate the lot of

---

[3] Ibid.
[4] Ibid., 23.
[5] Ibid., 24.

the population." Commercial treaties had been concluded with many foreign states. Debt had been reduced, the deficit in the budget had steadily grown smaller, and by 1856 was almost extinguished.

Rayneval complimented the expansion of trade, home building, hospital administration, reforestation, and railway construction in the States. Numerous public works were carried out, including the drainage of marshes, the completion of railroads and telegraphs. Agriculture was encouraged.

> "There is, in truth, misery here as elsewhere," Rayneval reported, "but it is infinitely less heavy than in less favored climates. Necessities are obtained cheaply. Private charity is largely exercised. Establishments of public charity are numerous and effective."[6]

He particularly praised the prisons of the Papal States: "Some of these prisons should be visited, that the visitor may admire — the term is not too strong — the persevering charity of the Holy Father."[7]

By contrast, the prisons in Piedmont were, despite Cavour's loud promises of reform, quite literally squalid hellholes men were cast in to die.[8] Moreover, Cavour ramped up Piedmont's taxes and introduced conscription to build his war machine. Pius IX, on the other hand, banned forcing his subjects into military service even when his States were under siege.

Rayneval further observed:

> People have had ears only for the declarations of the discontented, and the permanent calumnies of the bad portion of the Piedmontese press... in spite of well-established facts it is believed in most places, and particularly

---

[6] Hales, *Pio Nono*, 157.
[7] Ibid.
[8] Smith, *Italy: A Modern History*, 123–124.

in England, that the Pontifical Government
has done nothing for its subjects, and has
restricted itself to the perpetuation of errors of
a bygone age.[9]

Rayneval continued:

Are we then to be told the Pontifical government
is a model, that it has no weaknesses or imperfections? Certainly not, but its weaknesses and
imperfections are of the same kind as are met
with all governments, and even in all men, with
a very few exceptions.[10]

Rayneval concluded his immensely unpopular report
with: "The pontifical administration bears the marks of
wisdom, reason, and progress."[11]

Although Rayneval's report was intended for private view-
ing by Napoleon and his close officials, it was published
in France and England. The reaction was an embarrassed
silence. Even Cavour seemed at a loss for words. Napoleon
III rewarded Rayneval for his honesty by shipping him off
to St. Petersburg. His report was not mentioned in polite
company. Focus was quickly directed elsewhere.

THE ROBE

Like his predecessors, Pope Pius IX took an oath to hand
over the Papal States intact to his successor. Yet more than
his oath was at stake in defending his States. Pius was born
and raised in the Papal States and served there as bishop,
archbishop, and cardinal before being elevated to the papacy.
He had a fervent love of his homeland, and when he became
Pope his love developed a mystical depth.

Pius believed the Church had been given the Papal States
by God to better fulfill her spiritual mission by keeping its

---

[9] O' Clery, *The Making of Italy*, 25.
[10] Ibid., 27.
[11] Hales, *Pio Nono*, 157

government separate from other powers. He reasoned that just as it would be a sacrilege to secularize a cathedral, so would it be sacrilege to secularize the Papal States — a territory set apart by God for a specific spiritual purpose.

Well aware of Piedmont's ambitions, Pio Nono admonished King Victor Emmanuel for his complicity in Cavour's plotting. He reminded Victor that he was the "offspring of the illustrious House of Savoy", and exhorted him to "declare openly that you will not confiscate the goods of others, and much less a part of the robe of Jesus Christ, which remained whole even on the hill of Calvary." [12]

For Pius IX, then, the Papal States robed the Mystical Body of Christ. This was incomprehensible to Cavour and Napoleon, steeped as they were in the secular politics of plot, counterplot, ambition, and acquisition.

In 1857 Pius IX, now sixty-five years of age, repeated the pilgrimage to Loreto he made as a young man to seek a cure for his epilepsy. Now he went to entrust his spiritual children to the Mother of God. He toured his homeland, the Papal States.

The unexpected presence of the pope drew enthusiastic crowds of the "common people" who, despite the subversion of the revolution, still loved Pius as best they could. Stopping at his birthplace, Sinigaglia, Pius declined his bishop's offer of palace lodging to spend the night in the home he was born in — the home where both his parents had died.

As he walked through the rooms, touching the walls and furniture, perhaps he remembered how, as a boy, he had knelt with his mother for nightly prayers, asking Jesus and Mary to please help the Holy Father. Now an old man, he knew intimately just how much prayer the Holy Father needed.

He continued on to Spoleto, then Bologna. He was pelted with flowers, touched, caressed, and hugged as he came to his people. He was their pope, their king, and their

---

[12] Hales, *Pio Nono*, 200–201.

kinsman, and they received their hero with love, reverence, laughter, and tears.

Pius IX was already regarded as a saint, and after his tour more tales would be added to the catalog of miracles gained through his intercession. In those sunny days of 1857 the revolution fled the light and bided its time. For the children of the City of God, it may have seemed Pius IX would always be pope, and that it would always be summer.

Or maybe everyone knew they were saying goodbye. For this would be Pius' farewell tour of the land where he was born and raised, the land where he served God, the land that had for centuries robed the Church and protected her spiritual independence. In a few short years, the Church would be stripped of the "robe of Jesus Christ."

The villain of the piece would be the recurring figure of Judas, now in the guise of Piedmont—a formerly great Catholic nation that still retained the cross on its flag.

The cross of Piedmont had been hollowed out and was now a Trojan horse bearing the Revolution in all its destructive, secularizing glory. This cross would bid fair to overshadow the cross of Christ, borne now by His Mystical Body. The robe would soon be gone. And the people?

° °

CHAPTER 17

THE AGREEMENT AT PLOMBIÈRES

E NTER Piedmont's Prime Minister, Count Camillo Cavour — the man most responsible for wresting the Papal States from the Church.

Cavour's original last name was Benso. The *Cavour* moniker came from an ancestor, Michele Benso, who received the title of Marquis of Cavour,[1] making him Michele Benso di Cavour, or Cavour for short.

Born under the rule of Bonaparte in 1810, Camillo was placed in a military academy as a boy. He had a great aversion to this environment. His impatience with the military led to his discharge and a disgraceful return home — an event that caused no mourning. At age twenty, Camillo wrote to a friend: "I have a great deal of ambition, an enormous ambition indeed; in my daydreams I already see myself Minister of Italy."[2]

After a long period of travel and study, Cavour was elected to the Piedmontese Parliament in 1848 — the year of the Roman Revolution. He aligned himself with the dominant Liberal party and joined many other legislators bent on limiting the Church's spiritual jurisdiction in Piedmont (Sardinia).[3]

Cavour became prime minister of Piedmont in 1852, just as he had imagined so many years ago. Suppression of the Church in Piedmont increased. The Jesuits were expelled. Legislation was passed barring religious orders from purchasing property in Piedmont. Priests were imprisoned, and Catholic professors were driven from their university chairs. In 1855, the government passed a law suppressing all existing

---

[1] Cavour was a small town in the metropolis of Turin, Italy.
[2] O'Clery, *The Making of Italy*, 2
[3] The names Piedmont and Sardinia are interchangeable. Piedmont is primarily used here.

convents and monasteries, then seized their properties. Such
wholesale robbery became as natural to Cavour as breathing.

In 1858 Cavour saw three enemies: Austria; the Catholic
Church; and radicals like Mazzini, Garibaldi, and Orsini.
The radicals were willing to burn it all down to "unify" Italy,
but Cavour wanted to preserve everything so he could possess it — thus gaining power and money, in that order.

"UNIFICATION"

Years before the "Mortara Affair" Cavour was sizing up the
Papal States for invasion and secularization under the guise
of "unifying" Italy. The word is in quotation marks because
the "unification" of Italy was code for the secularization and
domination of the various peoples and regions of Italy under
one centralized government (Piedmont-Sardinia), even if
the people did not want it — which they definitely did not.

This centralized government would, of course, be run
either by the Revolution or by more respectable politicians
who either shared the ideals of the Revolution or were too
craven to oppose them. The price of unity was high taxes,
conscription for wars, and a host of other unpleasant require-
ments intentionally not mentioned in the same breath as the
glorious word "unification." Recall Mazzini's counsel:

> There are regenerative words which contain all
> that need be often repeated to the people... The
> essential thing is that the goal of the great revolu-
> tion be unknown to them: let us never let them
> see more than the first step.[4]

Cavour's chief ally was Louis Napoleon III, former Carbonari Freemason and now Emperor of France. He ruled a
predominantly Catholic country — and had a quite Catholic
wife, Princess Eugénie. Consequently, Napoleon was not as
driven to secularize Italy — and steal from the Church — as
Cavour and the radicals.

---

[4] Maguire, *Pontificate of Pius the Ninth*, 26–27.

It was Napoleon who drove the Revolution out of Rome in 1849 after pressure from an irate French Catholic population. The Carbonari and Mazzini's Masonic *Young Italy* viewed this as an act of treachery by their former comrade. According to Masonic bylaws, traitors were to be "pursued incessantly in every place; and the guilty shall be struck by an invisible hand, were he sheltered on the bosom of his mother, or in the tabernacle of Christ . . ."[5]

ORSINI

Because Napoleon had less skin in the Italian unification game, he needed some encouragement to do the right thing. Felice Orsini was eager to oblige.

Orsini was a Freemason and former Mazzinian who had been granted amnesty by Pius IX upon becoming pope. He saw Napoleon as a traitor to the cause and a target for revolutionary justice. On January 14, 1858, Orsini planted three bombs that exploded near the emperor's carriage as it pulled up to Rue Le Peletier to see Rossini's *William Tell.*

The ferocity of the explosions killed eight Parisians and wounded 142 bystanders. Remarkably, Napoleon and Eugénie suffered only superficial shrapnel wounds. Orsini suffered more injuries setting off the bombs than his targets did.

To quell public panic, the royal couple attended the show as if nothing had happened. From prison, Orsini wrote Napoleon several letters, one of which was published in the press. It read, in part:

> Remember that, so long as Italy is not independent, the peace of Europe and Your Majesty is but an empty dream . . . Set my country free, and the blessings of twenty-five million people will follow you everywhere and forever.[6]

---

[5] Ibid., 27.
[6] John Julius Norwich, *The Middle Sea: A History of the Mediterranean* (New York: Vintage Books, 2006), 523. Orsini was remarkably bombastic in speaking as if all of Europe supported his revolutionary cause.

THE PLOMBIÈRES AGREEMENT

Cavour initially thought an assassination attempt on the French Emperor by an Italian would destroy his alliance with Napoleon. Instead, the bomb explosions were the encouragement Napoleon needed to become a more active ally of Cavour.

Six months after Orsini's attack, the two had a secret meeting in Plombières, a fashionable resort town in eastern France. They sat in a carriage that slowly clopped around Plombières again and again while Napoleon and Cavour plotted geopolitical strategy. After much discussion, a tentative agreement was reached. Nothing was put in writing, but Cavour later wrote a letter to King Victor Emmanuel detailing the meeting.

Since later events mirrored Cavour's letter, we may believe what Cavour said about Plombières. He and Napoleon III planned to provoke a war with Austria, then combine forces to push Austrian troops out of Italy. The first step in the unification of Italy was to get Austria out of the way.

Piedmont would repay Napoleon by ceding the Italian border territories Nice and Savoy to France. Napoleon further stipulated that his cousin, Prince Napoleon, wed Victor Emmanuel's fifteen-year-old daughter, thus uniting the royal houses of France and Piedmont.

In return Napoleon would allow Cavour's armies to carve up the Papal States, annexing them piece by piece to Piedmont.[7] Napoleon would not interfere with this process. This was the second step in the unification of Italy.

Anticipating the outrage of French Catholics, Napoleon stipulated that Pius be named president of the new Italian confederation — a point Cavour likely conceded with a nod and a wink, as both men knew who would *really* be ruling Italy.

---

[7] Denis Mack Smith, *Cavour* (New York: Alfred A. Knopf, 1985), 141-143.

IMPACT OF THE MORTARA AFFAIR

Plombières began on July 11, 1858. Edgardo Mortara was taken from his home two weeks prior, on June 25, 1858. It is likely neither Napoleon nor Cavour knew about Edgardo's removal while at Plombières.

News in the nineteenth century traveled as slowly as the horse-drawn carriage circling Plombières. It is more likely the triggering event for the seizure of the Papal States was the agreement at Plombières, not the Mortara Affair.

Certainly, Cavour did not mention the Mortara Affair to Victor Emmanuel. His letter has been translated into many languages, and he did not write the word "Mortara" in any of them.

Moreover, even before the Mortara case, Cavour had publicly "arraigned the pontifical government on the double charge of incapacity and oppression,"[8] the remedy being secularization and the Napoleonic Code.

As seen in the previous chapter, the Papal States were no less efficiently governed than Piedmont. Certainly taxes were much lower, and the prisons more humane. Cavour knew all this. His real foe was the temporal authority of the pope, but he needed a pretext to illegally seize the Church's large properties.

For the Church's enemies, "the taking of the Mortara boy was manna from heaven,"[9] and Cavour eagerly joined what historian Daniel-Rops called:

> A furious press campaign, in which all contemporary liberal elements took part, began in Italy, France, Germany, and England. It was joined by Freemasonry, to which Mazzini, Garibabldi, and many other leaders of Young Italy belonged.[10]

But before all this, there were Cavour and Napoleon circling around Plombières, plotting strategy. It was an

---

[8] Ibid., 20.
[9] Kertzer, *The Kidnapping of Edgardo Mortara*, 118.
[10] Daniel-Rops, *The Church in an Age of Revolution*, 269.

intricate conspiracy that Pius IX was well aware of. The
French ambassador to the Vatican found this out during an
uncomfortably frank meeting with the Holy Father. After
relating with precision the pair's plot to drive out Austria
and steal papal territory, Pius

> accused the French of planning to go even further
> than this and annex other portions of the Papal
> States to Piedmont, including the kingdom of the
> Two Sicilies and the duchies—Tuscany, Modena,
> Parma—leaving the Pope to rule only the city of
> Rome.[11]

A recurring criticism of Blessed Pius IX is that he was
politically naive, a political blunderer, or both. This may
have been true prior to the Roman Revolution—but not
afterward, as evidenced by his acute analysis noted above.
What Pius predicted was precisely what came to be, except
that Rome was taken from him too.

Then there is criticism about Pius' absolute refusal to
return Edgardo Mortara to his family, in the face of virtually
unanimous, very vocal opposition from world leaders and
the international press. This decision is viewed as evidence
of Pius' poor political judgment.

On one level this is accurate criticism. How simple it
would have been for the pope to earn the applause of the
world, disarm his enemies, and perhaps even preserve (for
a time) the Papal States by blaming the Mortara case on an
overzealous inquisitor and returning the boy to his heartsick
parents. Why didn't he?

---

[11] Kertzer, 121.

· ·

CHAPTER 18

PIO NONO AND PIO MARIA

Pio Nono was relaxing in Anzio when he chanced upon a French ship, the Météor, docked during a scientific cruise. One thing led to another, and soon the Pope was seated in an armchair on deck, blessing the crew.

Accepting the captain's invitation to join the day's cruise, Pius scrutinized the ship, asking informed questions about the various scientific instruments on board. At dinner Pius insisted on eating with the sailors in the mess room. He entered the mess and ordered the food servers to be seated. Then the Holy Father began serving the food, putting the astonished sailors at ease by laughing and talking all the while.

At days end, Pius was rowed to shore in a boat too large to reach the beach. The sailors fought each other for the honor of jumping into the water and linking arms to fashion a human chair, which carried Pius high and dry to shore.[1]

THE movie about the Mortara case, released in 2023,[2] gives everyone's view of the situation except for the Church's. Does the Church have a case? Does the movie's depiction of Pius IX as a fearful, paranoid, deranged fanatic truly reflect reality?

Strictly speaking, the internal affairs of the papal government — which was what the Mortara case fell under — were really none of the world's business. However much one may sympathize with their sorrow, the Mortaras intentionally and repeatedly (for years) violated the law of the land they lived in. They fully knew the consequences of their violation.

---

[1] Thornton, *Cross Upon Cross*, 164-165.
[2] *Kidnapped: The Abduction of Edgardo Mortara*, directed by Marco Bellocchio (2023; Italy: The Match Factory, Kavac Film, and IBC Movie, distributed by 01 Distribution), film.

On the other hand, even if the Mortaras violated the law, the punishment of losing their child was severe and unjust. The Church was a power-hungry corporation willing to break up families to increase membership. Looking at the past through the lens of today's secularized world, this conclusion makes sense.

Yet there is always a distortion factor when we judge the past by contemporary standards. However satisfying that exercise may be, it will always be inaccurate unless we understand the unique motivations of historical figures — motivations that always relate to and arise from the precise time they lived in, and what *their* beliefs — *not ours* — were; what their world was really like over 150 years ago, and what everyone back then believed to be true.

Accordingly, if the Mortaras believed the law was unjust they were free to leave the Papal States. If they chose to remain, could they reasonably expect the law of the States and canon law to be changed to suit them alone, and not the many other Jewish families who had the same experience?[3]

Was the Church overreaching? Grasping? Desperate for members? Just another greedy corporation hunting for wallets? Or was it a divinely instituted organization created to help souls get to heaven? A grace-filled reservoir of hope for the lost and forsaken? A body that believed the Sacrament of Baptism indelibly marked a soul for Jesus, and that that mark, that soul, must be protected, nurtured, and taught so that it could get to heaven one day? To forget the spiritual dimension is to lose an accurate picture of events.

A small consolation was the Mortaras' ability to visit Edgardo in Rome whenever they wanted. They visited Rome often, and by Edgardo's own account saw him every day they were there.

Recall Pio Nono's lifelong vigilance for spiritual orphans. His first "parish" was *Tata Giovanni*, a Roman orphanage

---

[3] This was the argument made in pamphlets supporting the Church's position, as quoted in Kertzer, *The Kidnapping of Edgardo Mortara*, 133.

for boys. Father Mastai-Ferretti spent years teaching ragged, dirty lads "to be useful to man and faithful to God."

He became devoted to his boys, and they to him. Many years later, a witness recalled the day Father Mastai had to leave *Tata Giovanni:*

> A cry of real pain ran from one end of the hall to the other. There were a hundred and twenty of us, large and small, and there was not one who was not crying bitterly. Suddenly we all started to rush to his arms. Some kissed his hands, some grasped his robe, those who could not reach him called him by every endearing name, as we all implored him not to forsake us.[4]

Did Father Mastai remain aloof from their sentiments? Did he distance himself from the mourning of children who now felt "doubly orphaned"? His former charge continued:

> He himself was so touched by our despair that he began to weep. He pressed the nearest to his heart, saying: "I would never have believed that our parting would be so sad." Then he tore himself from us and ran up to his room. He tried to shut the door, but could not.
>
> We were all there and made our way in. That night no one went to bed. We all remained in his room, and he spoke words I cannot describe, seeking to calm and comfort us. He told us always to fulfill our duties with joy and to be ever submissive to the decrees of Providence.[5]

PIO NONO AND PIO MARIA

His fatherly concerns only expanded when he became pope, as did his submission to the decrees of Providence. Pius told French journalist Louis Veuillot that "there was

---

[4] Shea, *The Life of Pope Pius IX* (New York: Thomas Kelly, 1877), 25.
[5] Ibid., 29–30.

no [political] danger so great that it would make him give
in" and return Edgardo Mortara, "because the Vicar of Jesus
Christ has nothing more precious than the souls who belong
to Jesus Christ."[6]

Some claim this attitude was political suicide for Blessed
Pius IX. They have a point. The problem was that he was a
principled man dealing with unprincipled men, governments,
and press organs. He was very unlikely to prevail playing
clean when everyone else played dirty.

But it is a mistake to call Pius naive. He knew it wouldn't
end well, but for him, principles were more important than
politics. If by today's standards this makes Pius "deranged,"[7]
he would have had a hearty laugh about this depiction.

Pius first met Edgardo shortly after the boy arrived in
Rome. "He received me with great kindness, and declared
himself my adoptive father, which he really was," Edgardo
Mortara would testify later.[8]

Polish Bishop Joseph Pelczar recalled Pius IX "clutching
the boy affectionately to his breast" and making "the sign of
the Cross on his forehead."[9] For Pius, abandoning a newly
baptized Christian would have been a mortal sin. For the
rest of his life he took personal responsibility for Edgardo's
Christian education and welfare.

It seems an even more highly placed personage than Pius
IX was also concerned with Edgardo's welfare. Perhaps this
was why the first Christian prayer he learned was the *Ave
Maria.* When Edgardo arrived in Rome, he was seen staring
at a large portrait of Our Lady of Sorrows.

---

[6] Kertzer, *The Kidnapping of Edgardo Mortara*, 158.

[7] *Kidnapped: The Abduction of Edgardo Mortara*, review by Matt Zoller
Seitz, *RogerEbert.com*, May 24, 2024, https://www.rogerebert.com/
reviews/kidnapped-film-review-2024.

[8] *Positio super Introductione Causae*, testimony of Father Pio Maria Mortara, sec. 1654 (Rome: Congregation for the Causes of Saints, 1954),
trans. Zenit, September 20, 2000. Hereafter it shall be cited as "Mortara's beatification testimony."

[9] From Pelczar's biography of Blessed Pius IX, as quoted in Kertzer,
The Kidnapping of Edgardo Mortara, 68.

The boy asked who she was and why she was crying. He was told: *She is the Most Holy Madonna, mother of Jesus Christ, and she is crying for Jews who refuse to become Christians, and for all sinners.* "Then she is crying for me too," Edgardo said, and the full weight of these words seemed to sink in down to his toes.[10]

Later, Edgardo would enter the priesthood. He chose the names of his two patrons and was thereafter known as Father Pio Maria Mortara. His vocation is remarkable for many reasons, not the least of which being that the struggle for his soul was not fought merely by natural forces like the press and foreign governments.

Edgardo recalled two strange incidents just prior to leaving Bologna. He was with his mother in their apartment, which was guarded by the police. "Although it was broad daylight, I heard a shocking, seemingly inhuman cry," recalled Father Mortara. "I was so horrified that I grasped my mother, dumbfounded . . ."

The second incident also occurred just prior to his trip to Rome:

> I saw an enormous mastiff on the threshold, which had a gaze that I don't know how to describe, but disconcerting, almost human. I was terrified and let out a cry of fear. When my parents arrived to calm me down, they were amazed by my story, because there was no dog in the house.[11]

Mortara's sighting of the enormous mastiff recalls Alphonse Ratisbonne's recollection of a "black dog which bounded and jumped before me"[12] in the moments before he was overwhelmed by the vision of Mary.

In six-year-old Edgardo Mortara's case, it preceded his journey to Rome and, by his own account, a remarkable

---

[10] Ibid., 67.

[11] Mortara's beatification testimony, sec. 1669.

[12] *Conversion of Ratisbonne,* 70. How such a hound got into the Church of San Andrea delle Fratte and unseen by Baron de Bussières doesn't seem to have a natural answer.

transformation. Only eight days after arriving in Rome, his
parents visited him. Father Mortara remembered:

> As they had complete freedom to see me and talk
> with me, they remained in Rome for a month,
> coming every day to visit me. Needless to say,
> they tried every means to get me back—caresses,
> tears, pleas and promises. Despite all this, I never
> showed the slightest desire to return to my family,
> a fact which I do not understand myself, except
> by looking at the power of supernatural grace.[13]

A little-remarked-upon fact is that the Mortaras could
have left Rome with Edgardo the day they arrived, had they
promised to raise him as a Christian. Despite their grief over
losing Edgardo, they refused to do this—even to reunite
their family.

As for Pius IX, he was no stranger to the griefs of parent-
hood either. Pio Nono once introduced Edgardo to a small
group in this way:

> The great and small wanted to take this child from
> me, accusing me of being barbaric and merciless.
> They lament for his parents and do not think that
> I too am a father. No one sympathizes with me
> in the midst of painful trials, while in Russia they
> violently abduct so many of my children (Polish
> Catholics). I had the right and duty to do what I
> did for this boy, and if it were necessary, I would
> do it again.[14]

Pius was referring to the Orthodox Church forcing thousands of Poles to renounce their Catholicism—an invasion of
human liberty rarely remarked upon by those so indignant
over a single child in the Mortara case.

---

[13] Mortara's beatification testimony, sec. 1656.
[14] Ibid., sec. 1661.

. . . .

CHAPTER 19

THE WAR FOR THE PAPAL STATES

L ESS than a year after the Mortara case Cavour and Napoleon's war with Austria was waged as planned, and as Pius had predicted, Piedmont annexed the Papal State of Romagna.

Although Cavour was fond of the phrase "a free Church in a free state," his biographer notes that:

> The anti-clerical laws of Piedmont were imposed on the Romagna, and bishops who refused to cooperate suffered imprisonment. Cavour con- demned the "excessive" religiosity of those who continued to believe in the Pope's temporal power, and spoke scornfully of the "rule by priests."[1]

Religious liberty was proclaimed in Bologna, and the law against Jewish families hiring Catholic servants was abol- ished. Ironically, one of the first actions of the new govern- ment after announcing religious liberty was to curtail the religious liberty of Bologna's priests and to jail Father Feletti, the inquisitor who authorized Edgardo's removal.[2]

Pius IX refused to concede the taking of Romagna. He excommunicated everyone involved in the seizure including, it was assumed, Piedmont's monarch, Victor Emmanuel II, and Cavour. Since the excommunication named no names it was speculated that Napoleon III might also have been included.

This was probably stretching things, but Pius IX was, to say the least, mistrustful of Napoleon — and rightly so, as it

---

[1] Denis Mack Smith, *Cavour*, 204. *The New York Times Book Review* called Smith "the leading historian of modern Italy in the English- speaking world." Professor Smith was not an unsympathetic biographer.
[2] See Kertzer, *The Kidnapping of Edgardo Mortara*, Chapters 18–20. After a lengthy incarceration, Feletti was subjected to a show trial for his role in the Mortara case.

later turned out. Even though French troops still protected Rome, this protection did not extend to the Papal States. Pius resolved to form his own army to defend the States.

THE PAPAL ARMY

At this time the pope was mourning the recent deaths of his brothers, Joseph and Gabriel.[3] The arrival in Rome of volunteers for his army soothed a painful period in Pius' life, and "he made a point of meeting them all personally, of inquiring about their families, and of blessing them."[4]

There were many blessings, for in less than a year, he acquired about 15,000 volunteers. The majority were Italian. The rest were Austrian, Swiss, French, Irish, Polish, Spanish, Portuguese, and Belgian. Maximin Giraud, the young visionary of La Salette, joined the ranks. So did "de Cathelineau from the Vendee, with his band of crusaders who actually bore the crusaders' cross on their breasts."[5]

It was a modest force, capable of keeping an advancing Garibaldi from carrying out his vow to attack Rome but no threat to Piedmont's veteran army of 70,000 troops and other military assets financially supported by Lord Palmerston and the Rothschilds.[6]

Even so, Prime Minister Cavour complained long and loud about the "mercenary foreigners" who had "invaded" Italy. He termed the papal army a provocation—as if his illegal seizure of Romagna and persecution of the Church there were not.

Cavour's pattern of creating pretexts to achieve his aims should be clear by now. If the "Mortara Affair" had never happened Cavour would have found another pretext for

---

[3] Francis Thornton, *Cross Upon Cross*, 244–245.
[4] Hales, *Pio Nono*, 209.
[5] Ibid., 208–209.
[6] Cavour's own admission of Lord Palmerston's involvement in the *Risorgimento* is found in O'Clery, *The Making of Italy*, 173. For the Rothschild's contributions, see *The Making of Italy*. Corti is a sympathetic biographer.

invasion. He was a master of modern politics: as skilled a liar as any current politician and happy to resort to violence when it suited his purposes.

Consequently, in September 1860 Cavour orchestrated an "uprising" in the Papal States. He arranged for his own band of mercenary foreigners to enter the States to spread violence and mayhem.[7]

This "great insurrection," as the Turin newspapers called it—yes, the press was in on it too—was the pretext for Cavour to send Pius IX an ultimatum: disband the papal army or Piedmont would invade the Papal States.

THE BATTLEFIELD

Even the English press conceded these demands were unjustifiable. Before Rome had a chance to formulate a reply[8] tens of thousands of Piedmont soldiers poured over the borders. "Without a declaration of war," noted France's Bishop Dupanloup, "as if we still lived in the depths of barbarism, armed masses overran the Papal States."[9] Gallant and doomed, the pope's small army turned to meet the onslaught.

On one side were seventy thousand battle-hardened Piedmontese infantry with new rifles, cannons, and fresh horses. On the other side were perhaps ten thousand badly horsed, poorly trained volunteers with few rifles or cannons. Most of the papal troops had muskets of varying ages and a modest amount of ammunition. The majority had never been in a war—until now.

Their only hope was aid from the French or the Austrians. The Austrians, weakened by their recent war, could not help. As for France, Cavour had already cleared the attack with Napoleon III, who conveniently went on a sea cruise for the duration of Piedmont's invasion.

---

[7] This is generally admitted: O'Clery, *The Making of Italy*, 187; Smith, *Cavour*, 223–225; or Hales, *Pio Nono*, 210–212.
[8] The ultimatum was delivered on September 10; the invasion occurred the following day, September 11.
[9] O'Clery, *The Making of Italy*, 189.

In several bitterly contested battles across the states, tens of thousands of Piedmontese wore down and defeated vastly outnumbered papal forces. The largest battle was Castelfidardo, where 30,000 Piedmontese engaged a papal force of perhaps 5,000, and gradually overwhelmed them. Since most of the international press wished to believe the worst about the papal army, their heroism in the face of impossible odds is rarely told.

Typical of their bravery was the papal General de Pimodan, whose small company stubbornly defended the town of Loreto. When a bullet shattered his jaw, he tied his face together with a sling without dismounting from his horse. Later, Pimodan took a second bullet, and then a third. A fourth bullet ripped through his chest, and the thirty-eight-year-old leader, crying "God is with us!" finally fell from his saddle, as much from loss of blood as from his numerous wounds.[10]

He was carried away to die in the sanctuary of Loreto, which had been converted into a hospital. Most of the patients bore not merely one wound but had numerous wounds all over their bodies. They suffered patiently and died well. A young French soldier went to his reward after writing to his mother that he gave "his soul to God, his body to Our Lady of Loreto, and his heart to his mother and his native Brittany."[11]

Another wrote: "Long ago I offered to God and the Church the sacrifice of my life. Envy my happiness, and comfort my poor mother. Long live Pius IX, Pope and King!"[12]

These were the men defamed by Piedmont's leaders — and the press — as "foreign drunkards" and "miserable cutthroats,"[13] as "assassins" with "a thirst for gold and a lust of pillage."[14] Another perspective was given by a French priest

---

[10] Ibid., 202–3.
[11] Ibid., 210.
[12] Ibid., 210.
[13] O'Reilly, *The Life of Pope Leo XIII*, 375.
[14] O'Clery, *The Making of Italy*, 190.

who witnessed Castelfidardo and told his fellow priest, "Let us kneel before them, these men are martyrs."[15]

o   o   o

Another priest on his knees was the last Pope-King, who drained his chalice to the bitter dregs. On Christmas Eve of that year, Pio Nono celebrated Mass in the Sistine Chapel with 200 soldiers of the papal army. After recalling how the weak and helpless infant Jesus caused Herod to tremble on his throne, Pius said:

> Behold, I also, a poor and weak old man, despoiled of all, without help, alone and without support, cause fear to my enemies. In the midst of all my misfortunes I feel within me a confidence which is never shaken. I feel that I shall be assisted. When and how? I know nothing; it matters little...
>
> I wish it to be known that I shall remain constant to the last. Humanly speaking, I can do nothing; but *omnia possum in eo qui me confortat.* And you — aid me with your prayers.[16]

But the deaths of the generous, heroic young men he had known, and the treachery that doomed them seemed to afflict his father's heart almost to death. Before everyone's eyes he aged rapidly. "More than once he fell ill," Hales recounts, "and the belief was widely held that he could not live much longer."[17]

The following year, during Holy Week, Pius was celebrating Mass in the Sistine Chapel. As he rose to read the Gospel, he collapsed back into his throne, "and remained senseless for some minutes."[18] His enemies watched and waited to see if Blessed Pius IX would rise again.

---

[15] *CRC*, September 2000, online edition.
[16] Maguire, *Pontificate of Pius the Ninth*, 419–420.
[17] Hales, *Pio Nono*, 217.
[18] Ibid., 226.

CHAPTER 20

PIO NONO AND CAVOUR

TWO years after the Mortara Affair virtually all of the Papal States had been seized from the Catholic Church by force of arms.[1] This has led many to conclude that Pius' refusal to return Edgardo Mortara cost him the Papal States. A statement he made to Edgardo — "My son, I have suffered greatly for you,"[2] — has been interpreted as Pius' admission that his refusal to return the young Christian to his Jewish parents cost the pope his kingdom.

This logic appeals to those who see the loss of the Papal States as just punishment (were they religious, they might call it divine retribution) for Pio Nono's malevolent use of his temporal authority. The pope had no business trying to keep his subjects Catholic so it was only proper to steal his lands to separate Church and state and prevent other violations of religious liberty like the Mortara "kidnapping."

WHAT REALLY HAPPENED

Many who believe this also believe Pius IX was antisemitic. This is a curious attitude since, by their own logic, Pio Nono was willing to give up his kingdom for the spiritual welfare of one Jewish boy. How valuing the soul of a young Jew more than he valued his kingdom makes Blessed Pius IX antisemitic is far from clear.

Pio Nono's opponents are wrong about more than one thing. Not only was he "un-antisemitic," the Mortara case was not the primary cause of the loss of the Papal States.

---

[1] The Church retained Rome and the narrow strip of land surrounding it, known as the Patrimony of St. Peter, until 1870.
[2] From Edgardo Mortara's testimony on behalf of the beatification of Pius IX, sec. 1661. The entire quote is "My son, you are very dear to me, and I have suffered greatly for you."

The episode was certainly useful to the Church's enemies, especially the sensational, one-sided spin put on the story by the international press. But the Papal States had been up for grabs long before Edgardo Mortara was born. Napoleon had seized them first,[3] and then Mazzini, before Piedmont's violent invasion permanently wrested the large region from the Church. While the Mortara case was welcome grist for the Judeo-Masonic mill, the fact that the States were a theocracy doomed them, with or without the Mortara controversy.

Another misconception is that ideals of human dignity and religious liberty spurred Cavour and other European leaders to rally against the Mortara Affair. This was *not* the opinion of Rome's Jews, who, according to David Kertzer, felt "bitterness and anger"—*not* at Blessed Pius IX, but at

> the liberal press that had championed the Mortara cause. Those who so loudly criticized the Church for taking Edgardo were denounced (by Rome's Jews) as self-seeking opportunists, more interested in making their own political points than in winning the child's release and the family's happiness. While these critics cast their stones at the Vatican from a safe distance, Rome's Jews were left to bear the consequences of an irate pontiff...[4]

PIO NONO THE MAN

While these "consequences" never extended beyond the rhetorical, being face-to-face with an indignant Pius IX was to be avoided when possible. Make no mistake: the kindness of Blessed Pius IX was universally recognized, even by Marianna Mortara, who said: "Pius IX is so kind."[5] This was an

---

[3] In fact, Napoleon's incorporation of the States into his Kingdom of Italy was the seed that became the *Risorgimento*.

[4] Kertzer, *The Kidnapping of Edgardo Mortara*, 162–163.

[5] See Edgardo Mortara's beatification testimony, sec. 1685, and Kertzer, *The Kidnapping of Edgardo Mortara*, 84. Marianna believed that "if she

unusual statement from a Jewish mother who lost her child to Pius' Church.

Even a Gallican bishop unsympathetic to Pius was moved to record the following details of his *ad limina* visit with the Pope:

> His head, regular in its features, noble in its over-
> all bearing, is particularly distinguished by a face
> full of gentleness, exuding the most mild kindness.
> Nothing is more limpid and benevolent than his
> look, nothing more paternal and gracious than his
> smile. In his voice, which is not lacking in power,
> one detects a wonderful inflection of tenderness;
> in his words, as well as in the aspect of his face,
> one has the sense that he bears in his heart an
> immense treasure of love.[6]

While Pio Nono's personal warmth and tenderness — his *paternalism* — was most appealing, he commanded a full range of emotion. His powerful personality left more than one visitor wobbly and disoriented; one gentleman was so rattled he left by a window instead of a door and nearly flipped over the balcony.

Because Pius IX was formidable when aroused, one can sympathize with the delegation from Rome's Jewish community, who had their customary annual meeting with the Pope shortly after the Mortara Affair had ignited international controversy.

After assuring Pius of their loyalty, the Jewish representatives immediately began urging him to release the boy. The Pope was not in the mood. "You have given a wonderful display of your loyalty this past year," he retorted, "stirring up a storm all over Europe about this Mortara case . . . you have thrown oil on the fire."

---

had been able to obtain an audience with the Holy Father, she would have had her son back."

[6] The words of Mgr. Plantier, Bishop of Nîmes, as quoted in *CRC*, September 2000.

After citing instances where members of the delegation had, in the pope's view, given newspapers distorted or incorrect versions of the Mortara case, he declared:

> The newspapers can write all they want. I couldn't care less about what the world thinks...Take care, for I could have done you harm, a great deal of harm...But don't worry, my goodness is so great, and so strong is the pity I have for you, that I pardon you, indeed, I must pardon you.[7]

The Jewish delegation pleaded with him, insisting they had remained loyal even after Mazzini took over Rome. The pope remained unconvinced and reiterated his views so forcefully that one of the delegates, Scazzocchio, broke down and cried. According to Kertzer,

> The whole roller-coaster session had lasted less than half an hour. Scazzocchio was so humiliated by the tongue-lashing he had received that, it is said, he suffered a nervous breakdown. Apparently Pius IX heard about this and in later years, at the annual meeting with the Roman Jewish delegation, the Pope went out of his way to be kind to him.[8]

CAVOUR

Contrast the words and deeds of the supposedly antisemitic pope with those of Prime Minister Cavour. The usurper of Pius IX's temporal authority was considered enlightened because he employed several Jews. Yet of one such employee, Cavour stated, "He is most useful to me in order to give publicity to whatever I want to make known. I have hardly finished speaking to him when he has betrayed me."[9]

He had no better words for "that cunning old rascal Rothschild," of whom Cavour stated, "It would delight me to put

---

[7] Kertzer, *The Kidnapping of Edgardo Mortara*, 159.
[8] Ibid., 161.
[9] Rev. Denis Fahey, *The Mystical Body of Christ and the Reorganization of Society* (Cork: The Forum Press, 1945), 180.

a spoke in the wheel of that Jew who is cutting our throats."[10]

This was a reference to Piedmont's indebtedness to the House of Rothschild for financing Cavour's war machine at home and abroad. His biographer asserts Cavour was "planning a revolution across the whole of eastern Europe from Poland to Greece." He also invited Hungarian revolutionaries to Turin "to provide them with fifty thousand rifles and facilities for making Hungarian uniforms, while an American machine would be used for printing false banknotes" for revolutions in Austria.[11]

It was odd for Cavour to blame the Rothschilds for a debt he had willingly incurred. Quite often Cavour's words didn't match his actions — like his slogan "A free Church in a free state." Cavour ensured the Church's "freedom" by suppressing all religious orders, expelling the members, and confiscating Church property in what has been called a "wholesale robbery."[12] This was not new behavior. Cavour had begun trampling on the rights of the Church a decade earlier as a minister in the Piedmont government.

After Piedmont seized the Papal States anticlerical laws were applied with vigor and violence, just as they had been applied a decade earlier to the Church in Piedmont. The Jesuits were expelled and their property seized. Over one hundred episcopal sees were emptied. Bishops were driven into exile or imprisoned

> ... because they would not sing a *Te Deum* for the success of the invaders, because they did not show themselves favourable to the new state of things; often they were imprisoned on a suspicion of reactionary views, without being told what was the charge against them.[13]

---

[10] Count Egon Corti, *The Reign of the House of Rothschild*, trans. Brian & Beatrix Lunn (London: Victor Gollancz Ltd., 1928), 301, 304.
[11] Smith, *Cavour*, 228.
[12] O'Clery, *The Making of Italy*, 5.
[13] Ibid., 371.

While supervising this persecution, Cavour sought to persuade Pius IX that this was all for the good of the Church — that the loss of Pius' temporal authority would allow him to focus more on the spiritual aspects of the papacy.[14] The blatant hypocrisy of Camillo Cavour was as remarkable as it was typical.

In 1861 the new Kingdom of Italy was proclaimed. Victor Emmanuel II was declared King, and Prime Minister Cavour was the mastermind of unification. His star was on the ascendant. All that remained was for Pius to die and for Napoleon III to find a pretext to remove his troops from Rome so Piedmont could seize the city and make it the secular capital of the secular Kingdom of Italy.

Instead it was Count Cavour who died, quite unexpectedly, at the pinnacle of his power. In the last year of his life he experienced insomnia, recurring fevers, and delirium that rendered him unable to concentrate or think. It was rumored he had typhoid or malaria, or even that he had been poisoned.

His voracious ambition was matched by alarming bouts of delirium. After his excommunication Cavour experienced unpredictable rages, dark depressions, violent stomach cramps, fever, and incoherence. Believing the problem was a "surplus of blood," he applied leeches and had doctors bleed him. It didn't help.

When it became clear he was dying, a priest was called. Cavour told the Turin press he was dying a good Catholic. On June 6, 1861, Cavour's negotiating skills were put to the ultimate test when he died and entered judgment.[15] When Pius IX heard of his death he cried out, "May God be merciful with the soul of this unhappy man!" and said a Mass for the repose of the soul of Camillo de Cavour.[16]

---

[14] This argument became condemned proposition 76 in the *Syllabus of Errors*. Interestingly, Cavour's logic — such as it is — has been borrowed by contemporary conservative Catholics to excuse the violent seizure of the Papal States.

[15] Smith, *Cavour*, 232

[16] Hales, *Pio Nono*, 226.

. . . .

CHAPTER 21

THE SYLLABUS OF ERRORS

D URING the seizure of the Papal States and
Cavour's systematic persecution of the Church
throughout Italy, Pius IX released the *Syllabus of
Errors*. Issued on December 8, 1864, the *Syllabus* (catalog)
contained eighty premises of the emerging secular civilization that had been condemned during the pontificate of
Blessed Pius IX or by previous popes.

The most famous—or infamous—condemned proposition was number 80: "The Roman Pontiff can and should
reconcile and harmonize himself with progress, with liberalism, and with modern civilization."[1]

Note that Pius is not condemning all modern civilization.
What is condemned is the assumption that a pope must be
in harmony with it. Historian Daniel-Rops explains:

> [The Syllabus of Errors] could not be properly
> understood without replacing each of the eighty
> propositions in context. It would then be real-
> ized that Pius IX had not intended to reject the
> whole of modern civilization, liberty, and prog-
> ress in themselves, but that he was anathematiz-
> ing liberty, progress, and the modern world as
> conceived by unbelievers—as weapons of war
> against religion.[2]

Each condemned proposition contained a reference to
the papal allocution it was from, providing context. The
Church's enemies accused Pius of making a sweeping condemnation of modern civilization. This accusation was itself

---

[1] As noted previously, Cavour himself put this proposition to Pius in
his attempts to reconcile the Pope to the theft of his kingdom.
[2] Daniel-Rops, *The Church in an Age of Revolution*, 285.

a sweeping condemnation and proved nothing — except, perhaps, that the pope had scored a bull's-eye.

What annoyed some irreligious members of modern civilization was the precision with which Pius unmasked the liberalism of his day, revealing its anti-religious bias, its violence, hypocrisy, and its utter inability or unwillingness to live up to its espoused ideals.

When one read the *Syllabus* it was immediately and specifically clear what was condemned and why. While many of the condemned propositions arose from the persecution of the Church in Italy, other condemned premises concerned broader errors such as rationalism, pantheism, indifferentism, and liberalism.

Although the *Syllabus* was specifically addressed to the world episcopate, the secular press presumed to interpret it to its readers, Catholic and non-Catholic alike. This caused no small amount of confusion, particularly in France, where Napoleon III refused to allow its publication.

In America the *Syllabus* was met with incomprehension — where it was noted at all. The Civil War was raging, and Catholics and Protestants alike were sealing with blood their fidelity to the Republic.[3] This was a familiar pattern in non-Catholic lands; the State replaced religion as *the* indissoluble principle.

In a letter to Mgr. Plantier, Pius wrote: "The world is lost in darkness; I published the Syllabus so that it would serve as a beacon and put it back on the road of truth."[4]

Pius IX originally wanted to publish the *Syllabus of Errors* in 1854, in conjunction with the declaration of the dogma of the Immaculate Conception. He was dissuaded from this by advisors who thought — probably correctly — that

---

[3] Karl Marx was rooting for the North, the "Union," while Pius IX's sympathies were with the Confederacy. Pius had a correspondence with Jefferson Davis, and viewed Lincoln as a "tyrant" for not allowing the southern states to secede — something the American Constitution seemed to grant its citizens as a right.

[4] *CRC*, September 2000

the *Syllabus* would take attention away from the Immaculate. Pius settled for issuing it on the tenth anniversary of the proclamation of the dogma of the Immaculate Conception, thus placing it under the protection of:

> The Virgin Mary, Mother of God, who has destroyed all heresies throughout the world... sitting as Queen at the right hand of Her only-begotten Son, Our Lord Jesus Christ...there is nothing which she cannot obtain from him...[5]

PIETY, DEVOTION, LOVE

Pius ordered a replica of the grotto of Lourdes built in the Vatican gardens. He often went there when beset by tribulations. "Here lies all my hope, for of human hopes I have none," he declared to a bishop, adding: "Hail Mother of our God, Mary ever Virgin, Mary, blessed Gate of Heaven."[6]

Exhorting another bishop, Pius said, "My son, we are soldiers, and we must go to those posts where the battle is most intense. You love her greatly, our good Mother, the Virgin Mary. Therefore, have confidence. As for me, She sustains me. She will not abandon you."[7]

He had a private chapel, "where several times a day I go to adore the Blessed Sacrament." There he placed a smaller representation of the Apparition at Lourdes, saying by way of explanation, "If my soul is afflicted, if it seems to me that God is deaf to Our voice, I will raise my eyes towards the Immaculate. She will pray with Us, She will pray for Us."[8]

Those who saw him publicly worshiping the Blessed Sacrament remarked on his composure and piety. "He looked like an angel," Edgardo Mortara recalled, after seeing Pius at the Church of St. Agnes. "All eyes were fixed upon him,

---

[5] Pope Pius IX. *Quanta Cura.* Encyclical, December 8, 1864. Reproduced by The Remnant Press, 10.
[6] *CRC*, September 2000.
[7] Ibid.
[8] Ibid.

and his eyes were continually and immovably fixed on the Blessed Sacrament."[9]

To the horror of his advisors, Pius continued to visit cholera victims in local Roman hospitals. This was not a new habit, according to Bernard O'Reilly:

> We shall not be surprised to hear of the Pope's doing in his old age what he had done as a priest in his early youth — seek out in the cholera hospitals the worst cases of infection, and attend to them with his characteristic tenderness...he found a poor plague-stricken Jewess one day, and never quitted her, lavishing on her every care his charity could suggest, till she expired, while he was lifting up her head to ease it in its agony.[10]

These were the qualities of the man called "the living incarnation of Antichrist" by Italian revolutionary Giuseppe Garibaldi.[11] It is to Garibaldi we now turn.

---

[9] Mortara's beatification testimony, sec. 1684.
[10] O'Reilly, *A Life of Pope Pius IX*, 328.
[11] O'Clery, *The Making of Italy*, 370.

• •

CHAPTER 22

GARIBALDI AND THE ZOUAVES

Pius IX's fascination with developments in science and engineering led to notable encounters. The pope made a surprise appearance at the opening of a steel railway drawbridge spanning the Tiber River in Rome. He blessed the bridge (which is still in use today) and discussed engineering concepts in some detail with Lord Manners, England's Minister of Public Works. Taking his leave, Pius smilingly remarked: "Tell them, when you return to London, that the Roman Pontiff is not always in prayer, surrounded with incense, with monks, and with religious."[1]

G IUSEPPE Garibaldi's hatred of the Church was equaled only by his hatred of Pius IX. The enmity began, perhaps, when Garibaldi offered his services to Pius IX in the "Italy for the Italians" crusade against Austria and was turned down flat. Shortly afterward Garibaldi aided efforts that led to Pio Nono's exile from Rome in 1848. Then he led the defense of the Roman Republic against French forces seeking to restore Pius to Rome.

Publicly vowing to fight to the death, Garibaldi changed his mind when the French army arrived and fled into the night with a small army, half of whom quickly deserted him. Another loss was Garibaldi's wife, Anita.[2] Rather than allow her corpse to betray his presence to pursuing troops, Garibaldi left her body for peasants to bury. Her shallow grave was quickly discovered by roaming animals.[3]

Garibaldi's revenge came ten years later when, with an army financed by Victor Emmanuel, he invaded and

---

[1] Hales, *Pio Nono*, 163.
[2] Some sources say Garibaldi was already married when he married Anita.
[3] George Martin, *The Red Shirt and the Cross of Savoy: The Story of Italy's Risorgimento (1748–1871)* (New York: Dodd, Mead & Company, 1969), 361–362, 365–6.

conquered Naples. English battleships patrolled the harbors to quash uprisings by the citizens, who were not happy with Garibaldi's unannounced invasion of their lands.

Informing Neapolitans their worst enemy was the pope, Garibaldi set up his own government that, predictably, seemed established chiefly for destroying the Church. A historian of the period remarked:

> This hatred of Catholicism and of Christianity was the real motive of the onset made upon the Church... and it revealed the character of the movement. There was in their policy far more of the desire to destroy the religious orders, than even of the greed to possess their property, and more of a wish to paralyze the organization of the Church than to appropriate the revenue of vacant sees and suppressed seminaries.[4]

GARIBALDI THE RULER

This was particularly true of Garibaldi, who is often portrayed as a swashbuckling freedom fighter. Like many heroes of the *Risorgimento*, it was easier to adore Garibaldi at a distance. Up close, it seemed he couldn't build — only destroy:

> The government he offered continued to offend almost all Neapolitans in some fashion, largely by attempting too much too fast and by not paying enough attention to law and order. In the city, for example, he released ordinary criminals on the ground they were political prisoners, and the rate of crime rose sharply.[5]

An English eyewitness remarked: "The people who were wild with delight at the arrival of Garibaldi would now be equally delighted to get rid of him..." Since most

---

[4] O'Clery, *The Making of Italy*, 370.
[5] Martin, *The Red Shirt and the Cross of Savoy*, 602. Martin, a secular historian not unfavorable to Garibaldi, goes on to detail the usual persecutions against the Church in Naples that are so tedious and predictable they will not be repeated here.

Englishmen were infatuated with the *Risorgimento* and "ga-ga for Garibaldi," this seems an objective appraisal.[6]

His loosening grip on Naples persuaded Garibaldi to yield his rule to Victor Emmanuel. This was not an easy decision, as relationships between Victor Emmanuel and Garibaldi — as well as Cavour and Mazzini — were complex. Victor Emmanuel envied the popularity of Garibaldi; Garibaldi despised Cavour for giving Garibaldi's birthplace, Nice, to the French; Cavour hated and feared Mazzini, who held him in contempt; and so on.

Though these men often disagreed violently among themselves, when it came to attacking the Church their gears meshed quite well.

THE CENTENARY

In 1866 the September Convention was held, and the French announced they were departing Rome. Bidding farewell to the French general, Pius IX remarked: "We must not deceive ourselves. The revolution will come here. It has proclaimed its intention, and you have heard it."[7] Europe's press agreed, and "confidently predicted the Pope's power at Rome would not for a single year survive the withdrawal of his allies."[8]

On December 8 of that year, as the French evacuated, Pius IX announced an assembly of the world's bishops in Rome the following summer to celebrate the eighteenth centenary of the deaths of St. Peter and St. Paul. The universal Church rallied to his call. In an era prior to modern transportation and communication, some 500 bishops, 20,000 priests, and 100,000 pilgrims made their way to Rome over the next few months to celebrate the centenary.[9]

---

[6] Ibid., 603. When Garibaldi visited London prior to invading Naples hundreds of thousands of Brits came out to welcome him.

[7] H. E. Manning, *The True Story of the Vatican Council*, (London: Burns & Oates Limited, 1877), 31.

[8] O'Clery, *The Making of Italy*, 419.

[9] Ibid., 421.

The festivities gave Garibaldi hives. Calling Pius IX "a filthy priest," Garibaldi announced he would make Rome "the capital of Freemasonry"[10] and began marching north from Naples with his 12,000-man army.[11] Given the circumstances, visitors to Rome that summer were risking their lives. Yet come they did, to see the white-haired old man known as Pio Nono to everyone but Garibaldi, who called him "the Vampire of Italy."

Blessed Pius IX didn't seem to notice Garibaldi. Neither did the bishops, priests, or laity gathered at Rome. At times, gunfire was heard outside the walls as papal troops skirmished with revolutionaries. That Peter and Paul were martyred in Rome was a fact that must have struck many pilgrims to their marrow.

It was in this charged atmosphere that Pius IX declared to the world his intention to:

> hold a sacred Ecumenical Council of the bishops of the whole world, in which, after united counsels and labours together, the necessary and healing remedies, by God's help, may be applied to the many evils which the Church is suffering.
>
> From this, as we greatly hope, it will come to pass that the light of Catholic truth may diffuse its saving illumination in the darkness by which the minds of men are enveloped, so that they may see and press onwards, by the grace of God, in the true path of salvation and of justice...(and to) propagate and spread more widely the kingdom of Jesus Christ on earth.[12]

THE BATTLE AT MENTANA

Picture it: Freemasons were howling for Pio Nono's scalp just outside the walls, and his reply was to announce

---

[10] Daniel-Rops, *The Church in an Age of Revolution*, 289.

[11] An interesting mix of Garibaldian Red Shirts, Piedmontese foot soldiers, and a few units of English infantry. See interview with Father Paul Schofield, https://www.youtube.com/watch?v=Qi9GRsHmnlI.

[12] Maguire, *The Pontificate of Pius IX*, 519–520.

a Council—in a now defenseless Rome. To call Blessed Pius IX fearless understates things. He had enough resolve for the entire Church and his heroic faith was infused into the small papal army, which was defending its pontiff against a larger, better-equipped Garibaldian army with Royal Army troops in reserve.

The papal army defending Rome was predominantly Dutch and Italian, with representation from most European countries. The Zouaves derived their name from a brave indigenous tribe in Algeria that had fought French colonizers. Soldiers from this tribe formed an elite corps in the French army. Known for their baggy trousers and colorful uniforms, the Zouaves were fearless and fearsome fighters.[13]

Despite being provided money, guns, and ammunition by the new Kingdom of Italy,[14] Garibaldi hesitated outside Rome. Instead of attacking he sent some of his men into Rome with explosives. In October 1867 a violent explosion rattled windows in the Vatican. A bomb detonated in the barracks of the papal army, killing twenty-seven Zouaves and injuring many more. The Zouaves found the culprits and swiftly dispatched them. Upon investigation police discovered the explosion was part of an elaborate plot to kidnap, torture, and kill Pius IX.[15]

His plot partially foiled, Garibaldi dithered again before engaging the Zouaves in battle. It turned out he had reason to hesitate, for once the smaller papal army began attacking Garibaldi they didn't stop until they had beaten his army like a drum at Mentana and chased them out of papal territory.[16] Instead of entering Rome, Garibaldi once again fled from it.

---

[13] See https://zouavenmuseum.nl/wp-content/uploads/2016/10/ for more information.

[14] O'Clery, The Making of Italy, 424, 432.

[15] Brennan, Life of Pope Pius IX, 222.

[16] There is much misinformation about the campaign of Mentana. Most of it excuses Garibaldi's defeat and minimizes the improbable victory of the Pope's army. The most complete account of the battle I have seen in English is by O' Clery, The Making of Italy, Chapter

The first time he abandoned the body of his wife. This time he abandoned at least a thousand corpses, and left fifteen hundred of his Red Shirts as prisoners of the dreaded "vampire," Pio Nono.

The Pope visited the prisoners — not as warden, but as a priest. "Behold me, my friends," he said. "You see before you the 'Vampire of Italy,' of whom your General has spoken. What! All of you have taken up arms to rush against me, and you find only a poor old man!" [17]

More than a few Garibaldians wept and kissed his ring. Pio Nono clothed the ones he was able to and sent the repentant ones home.

The Catholic world was thrilled by the victory at Mentana, and the Revolution was stunned. There would be a Council after all.

XX. This very detailed report of the battle — almost a bullet-by-bullet account — not only gives the papal army their just due, it makes the difference between the forces of good and evil as stark as the Cross.

[17] Maguire, *The Pontificate of Pius the Ninth*, 456.

CHAPTER 23

HENRY EDWARD MANNING

GARIBALDI'S defeat stunned the Revolution. The papal Zouaves kept Rome free from invasion and won for its commander a brief window of time for the First Vatican Council to be held.

Having secured this, the Zouaves returned to their normal duties: policing Rome and her borders and aiding victims of a cholera epidemic. In their various roles the Zouaves at times appeared as guardian angels to those in need, be they the pope or poor Romans. Many Zouaves died of cholera while helping its victims.

Another visitor of victims was Pio Nono, who continued to horrify his advisors by regularly visiting Roman cholera hospitals. Pius ignored the highly contagious nature of the disease to hear confessions, administer anointings, and perform last rites. He shrugged off the danger: God would either preserve him or strike him, as He saw fit.[1]

It was during one of these visits that Pius heard of a Belgian nun in a Roman infirmary. The sister's right arm was completely paralyzed, and doctors were baffled. Pius visited the infirmary and engaged her in conversation. Eventually he asked her to cross herself with her right hand. Slowly, painfully, the sister did so. It was the first time she had moved her right arm in months.

Then Pius took a ring off the sister's left hand and placed it on her right hand. She felt a tingling in her hand and was shocked to be able to bend and move her fingers. Her paralysis was gone.[2]

---

[1] Pius visited cholera victims for decades as a priest, a bishop, and then as pope. It is remarkable — almost unbelievable — that he was never infected.

[2] Thornton, *Cross Upon Cross*, 199–200.

MANNING

The Gospel assertion "The kingdom of heaven suffereth violence, and the violent bear it away"[3] aptly describes the religious life of Henry Edward Manning. Born the last of eight children, the serious, solitary boy's destiny as a churchman was presaged by the nickname "Parson" given to him by an older brother.

At age eight Manning declared *The Apocalypse* his favorite book of the Bible: "I devoured the Apocalypse," he recalled, "and I never through all my life forgot 'the lake that burneth with fire and brimstone.'"[4]

He went to Oxford, where his forte was debate. So gifted was Manning at oratory he seriously considered a career in politics. The choice between religion and politics became a painful dilemma because Manning, an instinctive extremist by temperament, possessed an equally extreme ambition. Receiving no lightning bolt from heaven, it was Manning's will that finally wrenched him away from parliamentary politics and into the Anglican Church.

A cynic might say there was little difference between the two. "A damn large building with an organ in it"[5] was how some described the Anglican Church, which at times resembled a genteel country club as much as a church. Yet it was here Manning found the Oxford Movement and John Henry Newman. With a vengeance, Manning joined Newman's quest for religious authority.

Newman's well-known search began with his realization that the Church of England was no match for the secularizing fury of the Revolution. His courage in converting was considerable. Few places were as determinedly anti-Catholic as nineteenth-century England. Newman recalled being:

---

[3] Mt. 11:12.
[4] Robert Gray, *Cardinal Manning* (London: George Weidenfeld & Nicolson Ltd., 1985), 14.
[5] Ibid., 36.

...held in abhorrence...we are spat at by the
malevolent; we are passed by with a shudder of
contemptuous pity by the better natured...we are
regarded as something unclean: and our advances
are met as would be those of some hideous
baboon, or sloth, or rattlesnake, or toad, which
strove to make itself agreeable.[6]

In his *Apologia* Newman admitted wrestling with the
belief that the Pope was the Antichrist well into his forties.
By 1847 it was Manning's turn to wrestle. Newman had
converted in 1845, leaving his pupil poised at the cliff's edge
Newman had leapt from. Viewed now as a leader in the
Anglican Church, Manning's ambition screamed against the
religious and political suicide of converting to Catholicism.

Conversely, his extreme temperament reviled half-
measures in the search for truth. His will had only contempt
for the dilemma caused by his imperfections. Mercilessly, he
concluded:

The sloth and unprofitableness of my life are only
equalled by my vanity and self-complacency. I
have talked like a saint; dreamed of myself as a
saint; and flattered myself as I did the work of a
saint; and now I find that I am not worthy to be
called a penitent.[7]

During Lent he began bleeding from the mouth. His
health collapsed, and he was bedridden for three months.
Doctors examined him, consulted each other, and speculated.
Manning continued to scourge himself through Lent. Then
he recovered and went to Rome.

CONVERSION

Pius IX first saw Manning kneeling in a crowd as the papal
carriage coursed through the streets of Rome. Newman was

---

[6] Ibid., 100.
[7] Ibid., 115.

also in Rome at Pius' invitation. Manning looked so different after his illness Newman did not recognize him.

Manning stayed in Rome into 1848, the Year of Revolutions. He listened to public speeches given by the secret societies urging Pius to declare a holy war against Austria. Then Manning saw Pius close up during the Pope's Benediction of the Blessed Sacrament. On Pius' face was "a mixture of majesty, love, and supplication" Manning had never witnessed. "It was a sight beyond words," he remembered, concluding: "It is impossible not to love Pius IX."[8]

On his last day in Rome, Manning managed a brief audience with the Pope. Despite the oppressive political pressure bearing down on him, Pius was courteous and attentive. He asked Manning about Anglicanism and could not hide his scandalized reaction to Manning's answers.

On his way back from Rome, Manning stopped in Milan to view the body of St. Charles Borromeo, one of the leaders of the Council of Trent. Here Manning finally received the irresistible religious call he had longed for all his adult life.

He returned to England to flay himself for two more years, and to prepare his family for the shock of his conversion. For Manning's trip to Rome — and Milan — had clarified many things. He now saw Protestantism as "a chaos, a wreck of fragments, without idea, principle, or life. It is to me flesh, blood, unbelief, and the will of man."

Similarly, Anglicanism was "in essence the same, only elevated, constructed, and adorned by intellect, social and political order . . . it has so faded out of my mind that I cannot say I reject it, but I know it no more."[9]

Manning arrived at Catholicism after an unsparing internal struggle. Given the violent surgery he performed on himself, using his will as a scalpel to pare down the tumors of religious and political ambition, it was fitting that Henry Edward Manning was received into the Church on Passion

---

[8] Ibid., 125.
[9] Ibid., 131.

Sunday, April 6, 1850. He was destined to play as decisive a role at the First Vatican Council as St. Charles Borromeo, the saint who called Manning to the Church, had played at the Council of Trent.

o   o   o

Dark murmurings began in the press about violence against the Council. When Pius IX heard this he replied, "The Council will take place. This is what God wants! Should we be forced to leave Europe, then, if necessary, we will transfer it to Peking!"[10]

And so it came to be.

---

[10] As quoted in *CRC*, September 2000.

CHAPTER 24

THE VATICAN COUNCIL

BLESSED Pius IX formally opened the First Vatican Council in the presence of 700 bishops on December 8, 1869. Many of the poorer bishops had their expenses paid by the pope, causing him to joke: "I don't know whether the Pope will emerge from this Council fallible or infallible; but it is certain that he will be bankrupt!"

The Council of Trent defined doctrines denied by the Reformers. By the time of the First Vatican Council the very foundations of Christianity were being denied by the Revolution. Hence, most of the Council was spent debating and revising the first schema, *De Fide*, on the basics of the faith: the existence of God, revelation, and the difference between nature and grace.

The Fathers worked with painstaking care for five months, eventually incorporating 364 amendments into the text. On April 24, 1870, the Constitution (renamed *Dei Filius*) was unanimously accepted by the Council.

Dei Filius affirmed the existence and nature of God and revelation; explained the difference between faith and reason; clarified the relationship between faith and reason; and between faith and science. It incorporated the *Syllabus of Errors* in condemnations of atheism, pantheism, naturalism, rationalism, and materialism.

After confirming *Dei Filius*, Pius addressed the Council: "You see, beloved brethren, how good and pleasant it is to walk in the house of God in unity and peace...."[1]

---

[1] Gray, *Cardinal Manning*, 229.

INFALLIBILITY

Because the next schema, *De Ecclesia Christi* (On the Church of Christ), contained fifteen chapters it was obvious debate would not be completed before the Council adjourned to avoid the hot Roman summer. In March, Archbishop Manning petitioned to replace the two original chapters on papal primacy with four new chapters, one of which defined papal infallibility. Comments were invited and received on the new chapters.

In April, Manning organized another petition, signed by a clear majority of Council Fathers, requesting that Pius allow the Council to debate the four new chapters first. Modern Europe caught wind of the petition and waxed hysterical.

Earlier threats of violence against the Council led Princess Eugénie to pressure Napoleon III to send French troops to Rome. Now England and Italy pressured France to withdraw her newly arrived troops, which would leave the Council defenseless.

The Austrian ambassador ominously warned of the "irreparable chasm" a definition of papal infallibility would cause between the Church and Europe. This warning begged the deeper question: why had the European powers, under the lash of the Revolution, already forged a sizable abyss between the Church and modern Europe?

For example, England was aghast at the idea of papal infallibility and rallied behind John Henry Newman, who called proponents of papal infallibility "an aggressive and insolent faction." He further alleged that not only would a definition of papal infallibility be "most unfortunate and ill-advised," it could even significantly delay Christ's Second Coming![2]

England's agent in Rome asked Newman's counterpart, Manning, if anything could prevent a definition on infallibility. "Certainly," Manning replied. "Cut our

---

[2] Manning, *The True Story of the Vatican Council*, 97.

throats."[3] The "insolent faction" Newman referred to was the overwhelming majority of the Council Fathers. Even the minority agreed with papal infallibility but disagreed as to the timing of the proclamation.

The minority party was led by French Bishop Dupanloup, who organized a petition and sent a personal letter to Pius asking that the Council not define infallibility. Pius granted the majority's petition to debate papal infallibility. His reasons were several.

First, it was logical to honor a reasonable request made by a majority of Council Fathers. Second, Pius did not wish to see the conflict over the definition stretch into the fall of 1870. He knew war was now a defining mark of modern Europe; there may not be another chance to gather the world's bishops to Rome.

Last, and most importantly, Pius believed the doctrine of papal infallibility was validated by Tradition and Scripture. He believed Christ's extraordinary words to Peter—"I have prayed for thee that thy faith fail not; and thou being once converted, confirm thy brethren" (Luke 22:32)—were an inseparable part of the rock upon which Christ built his Church: a supernatural organization that would exist by benefit of the supernatural protection against error granted first to Peter, then to his successors.

This supernatural protection guaranteed that the Church, despite all outward appearances, was destined to outlast the Revolution. The infallibility of the Roman pontiff was a beacon in the storm for souls to struggle towards.

While scrupulously avoiding influencing the Council, this was the truth Pius hoped the Council would proclaim—not to assuage an aging pontiff's vainglory or to console him for material losses, but for the sake of the salvation of the world and as a refuge for orphans of the Revolution.

---

[3] Gray, *Cardinal Manning*, 233.

THE DEBATE

On May 13, 1870, the Council began the debate on papal infallibility. As previously mentioned, both sides believed the doctrine of papal infallibility; minority leader Bishop Félix Dupanloup's doctoral thesis was a defense of papal infallibility. Rather, the minority (about 140 of the 700 Council Fathers) argued that a definition was "inopportune" because there was no pressing need that mandated a definition.

They feared dogmatizing papal infallibility would drive away potential Protestant and Eastern Orthodox converts. They worried further about the reaction of European governments to the Church's claim of universal spiritual sovereignty. Lastly, they saw a tangle of problems in precisely defining the conditions and limitations of papal infallibility.

The minority's concerns were fully and repeatedly expressed for nearly two months. Everyone had their say, at length.

The infallibists, in turn, argued a definition was urgent, noting that the two years of public uproar over the issue had penetrated the Church and the Council. The majority felt a failure to define infallibility would be an unpardonable act of cowardice and sure to scandalize faithful Catholics.

They argued further that the truth of the doctrine required its proclamation, citing St. Paul: "Woe unto us if we preach not the gospel." (I Cor. 9:16).

In response to the minority's fears of driving away converts, Manning, the only convert at the Council, argued that defining papal infallibility would attract Protestants.

Generally, the infallibists were not overly concerned with political fallout over the definition. Many, like Manning, felt it essential to expose a backsliding Christendom to the full light of truth, to defend the faith, and to awaken wayward souls.

Although opponents of the Council later maintained the majority stifled debate, the facts do not support this claim. After weeks of argument, both sides agreed to limit and then close the debate.[4] Later a bishop from a liberal republic would claim: "Our Congress has not greater liberty of discussion than the Vatican Council."[5]

DEFINING INFALLIBILITY

Debate over the actual definition turned on two points. The Council stressed that infallibility applied to the papal office, not to the personal merits of a particular pope. Further, God's gift of infallibility was limited to the pope's exercise of his primacy: "when the teaching of the Universal Church is the motive and the end, and then only when the matter of the teaching is of faith and morals."[6]

A pope's prudential decisions or his statements made as a "private theologian" were *not* similarly protected. The dogma, then, is quite narrow. Infallibility applies only when the Pope:

> Speaks *ex cathedra*, that is, when, in discharge of the office of Pastor and Doctor of all Christians, by virtue of his supreme Apostolic authority, he defines a doctrine regarding faith or morals to be held by the Universal Church, by the divine assistance promised to him in blessed Peter, is possessed of that infallibility with which the divine Redeemer willed that His Church should be endowed for defining doctrine regarding faith and morals...[7]

THE ROLE OF BISHOPS IN INFALLIBILITY

The second point concerned whether the bishops had a role in papal infallibility. Must the Pope consult the Church prior to making an *ex cathedra* pronouncement?

---

[4] Hales, *Pio Nono*, 306.
[5] Manning, *The True Story of the Vatican Council*, 157.
[6] Ibid., 190.
[7] *Vatican Council I: Pastor Aeternus (On the Church of Christ)*, July 18, 1870, in *The Papal Encyclicals Online*, https://www.papalencyclicals. net/councils/ecum20.htm.

The inopportunists thought so and pressed for an explicit statement requiring prior consultation in the definition.

As a practical matter, popes frequently consulted the Church hierarchy on difficult issues. A century later, Pius XII would do so prior to infallibly defining the dogma of the Assumption. However, this was different from requiring them to do so. A small group of inopportunist bishops personally pleaded with Pius, on their knees, for such a concession.

Pius was sympathetic but directed the bishops back to the Council. The final wording on this point severed the bishops from any claim to papal infallibility: "... and therefore such definitions of the Roman Pontiff are irreformable of themselves and not from the consent of the Church." The canon of the definition reads:

We *teach and define* as a divinely revealed dogma that

- when the Roman pontiff speaks EX CATHEDRA,
    - that is, when,
    - in the exercise of his office as shepherd and teacher of all Christians,
    - in virtue of his supreme apostolic authority,
    - he defines a doctrine concerning faith or morals to be held by the whole church,
- he possesses,
    - by the divine assistance promised to him in blessed Peter,
- that infallibility which the divine Redeemer willed his church to enjoy in defining doctrine concerning faith or morals.
- *Therefore*, such definitions of the Roman pontiff are of themselves, and not by the consent of the church, irreformable.

So then, should anyone, which God forbid, have the temerity to reject this definition of ours: let him be anathema.[8]

---

[8] *Pastor Aeternus*, Chapter 4, emphasis in the original.

The constitution containing the new dogma, *Pastor Aeternus,* was overwhelmingly approved on July 18, 1870, the last day of the Council.

Outside St. Peters a violent storm darkened the sky. As the Fathers called out their votes thunder boomed and lightning flashed in vivid counterpoint. Pius confirmed *Pastor Aeternus* by candlelight, heedless of a glass ceiling panel that, dislodged by the storm, shattered near the papal chair.

Liberals saw the storm as a sign of divine displeasure. Manning likened it to Mount Sinai and the Ten Commandments. Yet the violence may also have been a snarl of rage from the prince of this world. The storm continued the following day, when Prussians and French began killing each other. It would rage unabated even after Rome had been conquered and Pius IX had become the "Prisoner of the Vatican." To paraphrase Napoleon: after the Council came the deluge.

. . . .

CHAPTER 25

THE FALL OF ROME

I T was rare for a pope to reach his fiftieth anniversary of entering the priesthood. Pius reached this milestone on April 11, 1869. Gifts and congratulations poured in from all over the world. Pio Nono celebrated the day in understated fashion, celebrating a low Mass at St. Peter's, then spending the day in audiences with rulers and ecclesiastics.

The next day he celebrated Mass in the humble Orphan's Chapel where he had celebrated his first Mass. Pius' lifelong concern for the welfare of young boys was shared by his friend, the holy Piedmontese priest Don Bosco. A few years later Pius approved Don Bosco's Salesian Order, created to further the education of young men.

For the Revolution, it was not just the Council's pronouncement of papal infallibility that was "inopportune." They were repulsed by the very idea of a Council. One can understand the reluctance of the Church's enemies to have their noses rubbed in Catholicism again. It was further proof of the Revolution's failure to "annihilate" (their word) the Church, the papacy, and religion.

After defining papal infallibility and papal primacy, the sky fell on Catholic Europe. France declared war on Prussia and withdrew her troops from Rome. Almost immediately the French army was routed in a series of battles. On September 2, 1870, Napoleon III and tens of thousands of his soldiers were captured at the Battle of Sedan, leaving France at Prussia's mercy.

Napoleon had been instrumental in "unifying" Italy, but when he called on Italy to aid him against Prussia, he heard only crickets chirping in the silence. There was no honor among thieves. The politics of expediency finally caught up with Napoleon III.

THE MARCH ON ROME

King Victor Emmanuel II lost no tears over Napoleon's fate, or time advancing on Rome. Within the week he informed Pius by letter that Italian troops would soon occupy the city. Calling himself Pius' "most humble, most obedient, and most devoted son," King Victor justified violating his pledge not to invade Rome by invoking the nobler goal of protecting Pius from the clutches of a revolution in Rome.

In fact, Rome was relatively secure from the Revolution. Mazzini's role had been subsumed by Piedmont, leaving him to lurk in the shadows seeking subversion. Garibaldi was once more in exile, and the Papal Zouaves were patrolling Rome and Lazio, the territory in which Rome resided.

The only threat to Rome in 1870 came from bombs and other acts of random destruction by agitators financed by King Victor's government.[1] Victor's use of professional violence while posturing as the restorer of civil order was the same tactic Cavour had used to seize the Papal States. Later, similar tactics would be adopted by leaders like Hitler and Stalin.

But for now, Victor wisely chose not to present his humbug to Pius face to face. This unenviable task fell to the king's envoy, Count San Martino, who personally informed Pius of King Victor's intent to occupy Rome to "secure Pius' personal welfare." Pio Nono's response could have peeled paint. He told San Martino that King Victor and his accomplices were "whitened sepulchers and vipers . . . I know you not, and will not know you."[2] He emphatically promised the ashen envoy that King Victor would never enter Rome.

---

[1] Martin, *The Red Shirt and the Cross of Savoy*, 715.
[2] Brennan, *Life of Pope Pius IX*, 243.

Pius assumed such a commanding presence and expressed himself so forcefully that San Martino was overwhelmed. He bolted for the door and, in his confusion, almost fell out a long window instead. Pitying the panicked count, Pius softened, smiled, and added: "But that assurance is not infallible."[3]

FINAL ACT OF THE LAST POPE KING

The Piedmontese army arrived at Rome on September 19 and pointed their cannons at the crumbling walls of the Eternal City. On that same day Pio Nono took a final walk through the streets of Rome. He stopped in front of the *Scala Sancta*, the Sacred Stairs Christ ascended to be condemned to death; afterward, He descended the twenty-eight Tyrolean marble stairs to carry His cross.

Eighteen centuries later His pope contemplated the Sacred Stairs. In full view of Romans and Zouaves, Pius — now seventy-nine and with snow-white hair — ascended the *Scala Sancta* on his knees. At the chapel atop the stairs, he wept and prayed in a loud voice:

> O great God! My Lord and Saviour! I implore Thee by the precious blood shed, of old, upon these very stones... by the anguish, by the sacrifice of Thy Divine Son, who willingly ascended these self-same stairs of opprobrium to offer Himself as a holocaust for the people who insulted Him, who were about to slay Him...
>
> Do not permit the sacrilegious feet of the enemy to desecrate Thy holy places. Spare my people, for they are also Thine. If there must be a victim, oh then, dear Lord, take me, but spare them. Sacrifice thy unworthy servant, thy undeserving representative. I am old; too long have I lived; let me be sacrificed. Mercy, O God, mercy! But come what may, let Thy holy will be done![4]

---

[3] Hales, *Pio Nono*, 314.
[4] Brennan, *Life of Pope Pius IX*, 245–246.

Pius descended the Sacred Stairs and, in the final act of a Pope-King in Papal Rome, he blessed his faithful Zouaves. Then Pius was swarmed by his people. Many begged him to stay, believing he planned to escape on a cruiser provided by former French Empress Eugénie. Others were distraught at the danger outside the walls and begged Pius to leave Rome at once. Calmly the pope blessed the crowd and consoled them with his presence. After soothing as many as he could, Pius returned to the Vatican. The palace doors closed. He would remain inside until he died.

THE FALL OF ROME

The last troop of papal Zouaves were driven inside the walls of Rome by the Piedmontese army, led by General General Raffaele Cadorna. The Zouaves reported Cadorna offered them arms and money if they would cause mutiny in the ranks.[5] The Zouaves were insulted and contemptuously refused.

Further dishonesty was practiced by Piedmont (Turin) press, which reported "the Romans had risen in their thousands, and blood was flowing the streets."[6] In fact, Rome remained peaceful. Historically, her citizens have been fickle about their popes, but as the sun set on papal Rome they displayed a fidelity to their leader that proved impervious to the temptations and inducements to betrayal dangled in front of them by the Italian army and the Italian press. Corruption truly was the coin of this new realm.

Outside the walls, Cadorna waited in vain for a revolutionary disturbance to justify his aggression, but his agents inside Rome had not even been able to put well-wishers on the walls. With a shrug, he ordered shelling to commence at 5 a.m. on September 20, as Pius was celebrating Mass. His resonant Latin was punctuated by the boom and thump of artillery and the rattling of windowpanes. After Mass,

---

[5] Ibid., 245.
[6] O'Clery, *The Making of Italy*, 513.

the fully composed Pope told a group of ambassadors he
had instructed the papal army to resist until Rome's walls
were breached. This would demonstrate to the world that
King Victor was not a champion of law and order but a
hostile invader.

The artillery attack breached the walls, killed civilians
and hospital patients, damaged churches, and set houses and
factories on fire Now there truly *was* disorder in Rome —
courtesy of the besieging army. As royal troops clambered
over the breached walls they encountered compact masses
of Zouaves, who repulsed them with gunfire.

The royals fell back and the battle ended. Zouave leaders waved the white flag of surrender. The Zouaves lowered
their weapons with tears of frustration. Most had spent the
night in the confessional, anticipating martyrdom. After
they surrendered, some of the Zouaves got their wish
when royal troops ignored the white flag and opened fire
on defenseless papal soldiers. After killing unarmed Zouaves, the Piedmontese picked the dead men's pockets.[7]

Adding further sheen to the glorious victory was the
presence of "scum" (O'Clery), "rabble" (Shea), or if you
prefer, a "swarm of human vermin" (Brennan) who followed the army through the breached wall and began loot-
ing property, desecrating churches, and attacking priests
and other religious. When complaints were made, General Cadorna is said to have replied, "Let the people enjoy
themselves."[8]

By *people* he was not referring to Romans, of course.
Rather, he gave full rein to the Garibaldians, Freemasons,
radicals, and criminals riding the army's coattails to enter
Rome and begin their curiously customary and ritualis-
tic routines of religious destruction. After decades of per-
sistent assault, the Revolution's siege of Rome was finally

---

[7] Shea, *The Life of Pope Pius IX*, 340; Brennan, *The Papal Zouaves*, 248;
Hales, *Pio Nono*, 316.
[8] Brennan, *Life of Pope Pius IX*, 252–253.

consummated. The thousand-year reign of papal Rome ended in an orgy of violence, theft, murder, sacrilege, and desecration. Yet another glorious victory for the Revolution.

THE ZOUAVES DEPART

Victor Emmanuel and his generals viewed the Zouaves as an enemy army no longer welcome in the new Rome. As they fell in line to leave, Zouave Colonel Allet was unable to contain his emotion and cried out *"Vive Pie Neuf!"* The roar that rose from the ranks of the Zouaves must have sounded in the breast of the old Pope for suddenly he was there on the balcony, looking down at them and raising his arms in a farewell surely heard in heaven: "May God bless my faithful children!" Overcome by emotion himself, Pius fell back into the arms of his assistants.

"Never can the enthusiasm of that supreme moment be equalled (writes O'Clery). With a frantic *'Eljen!'* a Hungarian Zouave draws his sabre; an instantaneous rush of steel is heard, and thousands of blades flash in the sunlight. The scene becomes absolutely indescribable.

> At the thought of leaving the Holy Father, tears of bitterest sorrow stream down the cheeks of men who had faced death in many a desperate struggle ... As the troops moved off, one last sad cry of *Viva Pio Nono!* burst from the head of the column, and caught up from rank to rank, was joined in, not only by the whole army, but by the crowd assembled to witness its departure.[9]

Many of the Zouaves killed in battle were buried in a cemetery adjoining St. Laurence Outside the Walls. Some were imprisoned, others were forced out of Italy, returning to their homelands penniless and on foot.

A large group of Zouaves boarded a steamer headed for France. One of the leaders had carefully hidden the white

---

[9] O'Clery, *The Making of Italy*, 531.

and yellow standard that flew high after the victory at Mentana. It was displayed in a solemn ceremony, and saluted with drawn swords.

> Then the flag was cut into hundreds of pieces, which were distributed to all present, for themselves and their comrades. Like the old regiment itself, the flag of the Zouaves is scattered far and wide over the world; it is "shrined on a thousand beating hearts," destined, I trust, to be once more united on some future day, when its veteran guardians resume their old place at Rome.[10]

---

[10] Ibid., 533.

● ●

CHAPTER 26

AFTER THE FALL

I T is rarely mentioned today but remains true nonetheless: Papal Rome was invaded without a declaration of war by a hostile army that seized it by brute force to secularize it. This violent aggression was championed by Europe's secular press.

How would the press have reacted if a papal army had surrounded Turin, invaded it, killed citizens and wreaked destruction, imprisoned Turin's government, and begun baptizing and catechizing one and all? To ask the question is to answer it.

Victor Emmanuel tried to justify the invasion by organizing a plebiscite (popular vote). The Piedmont army voted, and Romans stayed home by the thousands—those who had escaped the fate of most of Rome's civil servants, who were jailed for being sympathetic to the pope.

To no one's surprise Victor Emmanuel received ninety-nine percent of the vote. The plebiscite was such an obvious farce not even the *London Times* took it seriously. Perhaps the true will of the people is found in the facts that Victor never felt at home in Rome and was not welcomed there.

PIO MARIA LEAVES ROME

Prior to the vote a young Italian infantry officer named Riccardo visited the convent at San Pietro inside Rome. There he found religious novice Edgardo Mortara. Seeing the uniform, Edgardo shouted, "Get back, Satan!" "But I am your brother," Riccardo Mortara replied. "Before you get any closer to me," Edgardo said, "take off that assassin's uniform." [1]

---

[1] Gemma Volli, as quoted in David I. Kertzer, *The Kidnapping of Edgardo Mortara*, 263. Riccardo was several years older than Edgardo.

No more is known about the meeting of the two brothers. One can surmise Riccardo tried to convince Edgardo to return to his family—and failed. Edgardo continued pursuing his priestly vocation. Father Mortara never spoke publicly about his encounter with Riccardo, but he said this about the fall of Rome:

> After the Piedmontese troops entered Rome in those days of anarchy that preceded the formation of the new government, the police were unable to rein in the rabble-rousers. After they used their force to seize the neophyte Coen from the *Collegio degli Scolopi*, they turned toward *San Pietro in Vincoli* to try to kidnap me as well.[2]

The "neophyte Coen" was Giuseppe Coen, a young Jewish convert and aspiring priest. He was forcibly removed from his room in the seminary and placed back with his family. Giuseppe protested vigorously, but a court ordered the placement to continue. Upon coming of age Giuseppe left his family, returned to the Church, and became a priest.

How interesting the Revolution was so horrified by Edgardo Mortara being removed from his home, yet not only practiced their own "kidnapping" of Giuseppe Coen, but legally enforced their seizure of his person and violation of his will until Coen became an adult and was legally free from their aggression.

Because Edgardo was nineteen, he was no longer considered a child and could not legally be forcibly returned to his parents. Even so, Rome's police chief came to the convent "urging and pleading with me to return to my family, in order to satisfy public opinion," Edgardo remembered.

He also endured "the pleas and threats of liberal authorities who wanted to make me, in violation of my

---

[2] Ibid., 263.

religious vows, return to my family and expose myself not only to the danger of breaking my oaths, but, indeed, of becoming an apostate."

Edgardo said Pius IX gave him "the strength and the courage not to give in."[3] When it became evident his enemies would not stop pressuring him to leave the priesthood, Edgardo was quietly escorted from Rome and hidden in an Austrian monastery. Although he and Pius traded letters, Edgardo Mortara never saw his mentor again.

BELOVED POPE, BELOVED MAN

The world — and some in the Church — thought the fall of Rome meant the end of the papacy.[4] Nobody told Blessed Pius IX, however, and he continued being pope, which meant refusing to give an inch in principle to the enemies of the Church. A year after Rome fell, he wrote his brother:

> It is a true mercy of God this firmness He deigns to grant me in the midst of so many contradictions, so many evils, and especially their continual attempts to induce me to accept a policy of conciliation which is, of its very nature, impossible, since falsehood can never be confounded with truth.[5]

Persecuted and despoiled of his entire kingdom and temporal authority, the moral authority of Blessed Pius IX remained undimmed, as did his popularity. Historian Henri Daniel-Rops observes:

> Pius' misfortunes led to an enormous increase of his prestige ... the personality of Pius IX was undeniably responsible for a great deal of the

---

[3] Ibid., 263–264.
[4] Cardinal Manning believed the loss of the Pope's temporal power was a prelude to the reign of Antichrist.
[5] From Volume 2 of Fernessole's biography of Pius, p. 207, as quoted in Fernessole, vol. 2, 207, as quoted in "CRC Online Edition," September 2000.

fervour...all were struck by his charm, his affability, the noble simplicity of his welcome and that
sense of humour which seldom deserted him even
in his darkest hour...[6]

An example of this humor was Pius' response when a
nun asked him to autograph an unflattering photo of himself. Pius wrote over his bad likeness the words of Jesus
walking on the water: "Fear not, it is I."[7]

Even more than his humor, however, Pius IX's popularity was the product of universal heartfelt respect, admiration, and devotion for a noble leader who for decades
unflinchingly opposed a sea of underhanded enemies.

Seemingly single-handedly Pio Nono fought them all to
a standstill: liberals, Freemasons, socialists, Communists,
revolutionaries of all stripes, and their allies in the press.
Pius once told Louis Veuillot that all he could see were
blows aimed at him and at the Church. This continued
unabated in the last years of his pontificate.

The Church was persecuted in South America, in Mex-
ico, in Poland, in France and Spain, in Belgium and Switzerland, and especially in Germany. Pius IX never backed
down from any of these battles. Despite the grimness of
the struggle, he retained his famous sense of humor.

Upon becoming an octogenarian, he quipped, "I
carry my years so well I have not dropped one of them."
During the fearsome *Kulturkampf* in Germany,[8] Pius kid-
ded a group of nuns—whose faces were enclosed in very
extended round bonnets—by asking: "Whose faces are
those at the end of those hallways?"[9]

Often he was asked how he maintained his serenity amidst
the myriad tribulations of his reign. Once he replied:

[6] Daniel-Rops, *The Church in an Age of Revolution*, 275-6.
[7] Hales, *Pio Nono*, 329.
[8] Bismarck's systematic persecution of the Church in Germany, based
largely on the strategy Piedmont and Cavour used against Pio Nono
and the Church in Italy.
[9] Mortara's beatification testimony, sec. 1689.

My son, who ought to give an example of courage and constancy in the midst of tribulation, if it be not the Vicar of Jesus Christ? I suffer for justice; I am in tribulation for the Church; my conscience reproaches me with nothing. Behold the secret of my strength; behold the cause of my tranquility![10]

Father Mortara remarked:

He appeared majestic, without pretentious affectations. I had the opportunity to see him various times among the crowd that gathered around him to kiss his hand. He kept his gaze fixed forward, always seeming modest and detached, and seemed to dominate the multitude of people with his presence.

The thing that most struck me was the general state of his appearance. His blue eyes reflected the beauty and purity of his soul and the profound tranquility of his heart. A truly angelic smile blossomed on his lips. Joined with his normally benevolent and fatherly words, this made his appearance almost superhuman.[11]

None of the evils he faced could mar the greatest joy of Blessed Pius IX's life: his pronouncement of the Blessed Virgin as the Immaculate Conception. Heaven's response was to grace Pius with a vision of the Immaculate, and he wept when he beheld Mary in all truth. She would be with her beloved son until the end.

---

[10] Maguire, *Pontificate of Pius the Ninth*, 433.
[11] Mortara's beatification testimony, sec. 1689.

CHAPTER 27

. . . .

HEAVENLY PASSINGS

*A journalist once spoke with Pius IX about the continuing tribula-
tions of his pontificate. Perhaps the writer was trying to get Pius in
touch with his feelings when he asked, "Your Holiness, when will
these wretched things come to an end?" "I can't really say," Pius
briskly replied. "I'm the Vicar of Our Lord, not His secretary."* [1]

FATHER Marie Alphonse Ratisbonne's first visit
to Rome since his miraculous conversion coincided
with the last week of Pope Pius IX's life. Although
weak and ailing, Pio Nono insisted on giving Ratisbonne
an audience. The dying pope "fervently blessed Father
Marie, the Congregation of *Notre Dame de Sion* and all the
works connected with it, inquiring into every detail with
fatherly interest." [2]

Another coincidence was the date of the audience: February 1 — the same date as Ratisbonne's audience with Gregory
XVI in 1842. Pius remarked on this when he gave Father
Marie a painting of Mary: "Gregory XVI gave you a crucifix, Pius IX gives you the Blessed Virgin." It was a fitting
gift to be exchanged between two souls so devoted to — and
blessed by — Mary.

Father Marie spent the rest of the day "in blissful seclu-
sion" at *San Andrea delle Fratte*, the church of his miraculous
conversion. Later, he wrote:

> I found I could not say any vocal prayers...I
> began the "Memorare" over and over again. With
> beating heart and with tears, I thought first of one
> friend and then of another, asking, hoping, and at
> times utterly overpowered by my emotion. I like
> to think that in the midst of the joys of heaven

---

[1] Thornton, *Cross Upon Cross*, 189.
[2] *A Nineteenth Century Miracle*, 291.

we shall be better able to express our feelings. It
is too humbling![3]

THE RATISBONNE BROTHERS

Father Marie returned to Jerusalem. He was still there on
January 10, 1884, when the Fathers and Daughters of Sion
prayed at the bedside of his brother Théodore in Paris. An
eyewitness recorded:

> Silent tears are falling, the beloved Father's breast
> still gently rises and falls and his last breath escapes
> his lips so peacefully that the exact moment of
> departure is unseen... He passed from death to
> life without a struggle; the end was more like
> transfiguration than death. A heavenly expression
> settled over the peaceful features and the bystand-
> ers beholding it could grieve no longer... [4]

Four months after receiving the news by telegram Father
Marie contracted a fatal case of pneumonia. "I have never failed
to see the intervention of Mary in all that has happened to me,"
he said. "She herself is the hand of God — not the hand which
chastises but the one which pours out mercies — and that is why
I have never ceased to hope, even at the worst of times."[5]

There is no evidence he viewed his approaching death
with dismay. Instead, he anticipated it. "On my tomb," he
instructed the Fathers of Sion, "you will put only two words,
'Père Marie.' The first will describe the sinner I was, the second the Blessed Virgin's mercy towards me." On the evening
of May 6, 1884:

> A heavenly radiance lit up the features of the
> dying priest. He opened his eyes with a look
> of life and joy, an expression of surprise crossed
> his face followed by a radiant smile of happi-
> ness. This ecstasy lasted about three minutes,
> and then his eyelids closed, and his beautiful
> soul was with God... [6]

---

[3] Ibid., 292.   [4] Ibid., 323.   [5] Ibid., 294.
[6] *A Nineteenth Century Miracle*, 327.

Following the example of Blessed Pius IX, Popes Leo XIII
and St. Pius X favored the works of the Ratisbonne brothers,
including the addition of indulgences to this prayer:

> God of all goodness, and Father of Mercies,
> we implore Thee, by the Immaculate Heart of
> Mary and by the intercession of the Patriarchs
> and the holy Apostles, to cast a look of com-
> passion upon the People of Israel so that they
> may come to the knowledge of our only Saviour
> Jesus Christ and that they may share in the pre-
> cious fruits of our Redemption: *Father forgive*
> *them, for they know not what they do.*[7]

CATHERINE LABOURÉ

A generation later, a young priest was so moved by the
story of Alphonse Ratisbonne's conversion that he said his
first Mass at *San Andrea delle Fratte*. Father Maximilian Kolbe
also formed the Militia of the Immaculate, whose members
wore the Miraculous Medal and prayed to the Immaculate
for the conversion of Jews and Freemasons, whom Father
Kolbe called "the Church's greatest and fiercest enemies."[8]
Pius IX would have heartily agreed, it seems, since during his
pontificate he wrote eleven encyclicals against Freemasonry.[9]

The Militia's prayer was also something Pius IX (and St.
Catherine Labouré) would have endorsed: "O Mary, conceived without sin, pray for us who have recourse to Thee,
and for all those who do not have recourse to Thee, and
most especially for the Freemasons."[10]

St. Maximilian Kolbe never met Catherine Labouré. Neither did Blessed Pius IX. Father Marie Ratisbonne tried

---

[7] Three hundred days' indulgence was given according to the source
on p. 336 of *A Nineteenth Century Miracle*. Emphasis in original.
[8] Diana Dewar, *The Saint of Auschwitz, The Story of Maximilian Kolbe*
(New York: Harper & Row, 1982), 37.
[9] As well as "33 speeches and addresses and numerous letters to Vatican
dicasteries," all against Freemasonry according to *Inside The Vatican*,
March 2000, 51.
[10] *CRC*, no. 303, 5.

for years to discover the identity of the nun through whom the Immaculate had ordered the coining of the Medal that changed his life, but St. Catherine was so unbending in her determination to live a hidden life not even the Sisters of her own Order knew she was "the Sister of the Medal."[11]

She spent her last years caring for drunks and scrubbing stone floors on her hands and arthritic knees. When the Communards took over Paris in 1870[12] Catherine and her Sisters tended to the wounded, dispersing Miraculous Medals to Communist and Christian alike.

When she died her order buried her in a vault beneath their chapel. When her cause for canonization stalled decades later two old and crippled cardinals revived it. One couldn't walk. The other was a paralytic who could only use his right hand. With it he wrote: "The cause of Sister Catherine Laboure is the Cause of the Immaculate Conception." This seemed to turn the tide. After her beatification in 1933, her basement tomb was investigated and her coffin opened:

> Catherine lay there, as fresh and serene as the day she was buried. Her skin had not darkened in the least, the eyes which had looked on Our Lady were as intensely blue as ever, and — most remarkable of all — her arms and legs were as supple as if she were merely asleep.[13]

BERNADETTE SOUBIROUS

Another confidante of the Immaculate, Bernadette Soubirous, died shortly after Catherine and Pius IX. After Lourdes, Bernadette entered the convent of the Sisters of Charity at Nevers, France. There she received not visions, but trials,

---

[11] Dirvin, *Saint Catherine Labouré of the Miraculous Medal,* 225.
[12] And murdered the Archbishop (and many other religious) as the Immaculate had predicted to Catherine in 1830.
[13] Ibid., 229–230. Pius XII declared her a saint in 1947, noting: "She loved the Sacred Heart of Jesus and the Immaculate Heart of Mary with a special warmth of piety."

humiliations, and protracted physical illnesses that in 1879 brought her—at age thirty-five—to her deathbed.

Truly the Virgin had told Bernadette: "I do not promise you happiness in this world, but in the next."[14] She told her Sisters: "My suffering is to prepare me for heaven." When a Sister offered to pray that the Immaculate would console her, Bernadette replied, "No—not to console me, but to give me strength and patience." Pius IX knew of Bernadette's suffering and gave her a special blessing for the hour of her death.

The hour came, and Bernadette held the papal document in her hand. She spoke the special prayers. She clutched a crucifix to her heart and died praying the *Ave Maria*: "Holy Mary, Mother of God, pray for me a sinner, a sinner..."[15]

Years later her body was exhumed as part of her canonization proceedings. The crucifix she held on her deathbed still lay on her heart, coated with verdigris.[16] The rosary in her hands was almost devoured by rust. They were the only signs of corruption in the coffin. Eyewitnesses observed:

> Not the least trace of corruption nor any bad odor could be perceived in the corpse of our beloved sister.... The face was somewhat brown, the eyes slightly sunken, and she seemed to be sleeping.... The Superior General of the Sisters of Charity of Nevers and her religious moved the damp clothing and the sawdust mixed with charcoal which surrounded the body; both they and the doctor were able to testify to the fact that, although dried up, it was perfectly intact and bore no trace of corruption.[17]

---

[14] *Bernadette of Lourdes,* trans. J. H. Gregory (St. Gildard: Nevers, 1926), 254.

[15] J. B. Estrade, *My Witness, Bernadette, The Authentic Source Book of the Apparitions at Lourdes by an Eyewitness,* Reprinted 1951, Cahill & Co. Ltd., pp. 214–216.

[16] Verdigris is a green crust that forms on copper, brass or bronze after long exposure to air or moisture.

[17] See Franz Michel Willam, *Bernadette Soubirous,* trans. John Joyce Kempf (London: Sheed & Ward, 1933), 212., and *Bernadette of Lourdes,* trans. J. H. Gregory, 251.

° °

CHAPTER 28

OTHER PASSINGS

W E now know the body of Blessed Pius IX is miraculously incorrupt, as were the bodies of St. Catherine Labouré and St. Bernadette Soubirous. Their holy lives and edifying deaths are a contrast to the lives and — at times — abrupt and unforeseen deaths of Cavour, Mazzini, Napoleon III, King Victor Emmanuel, and Garibaldi.

As the decades of Pio Nono's pontificate lengthened, newspapers became prone to erroneously reporting his death. This happened so often it seemed the press was trying to will the pope's death by thinking about it a lot. Instead, they had to first report the real deaths of the leaders of the Revolution.

Prime Minister Cavour was correct that a benevolent theocracy could not survive the forces of modernized Europe. His chief claim to fame was the seizure of the Papal States to create the Kingdom of Italy. Another of his predictions — that Pius IX would not survive the loss of the States — proved incorrect. In fact, it was Cavour who perished quickly and unexpectedly (see Chapter 19).

VICTOR EMMANUEL II

Cavour's co-creator of the Kingdom of Italy was King Victor Emmanuel II, a bull of a man with sweeping sideburns and a flamboyant mustache swooping out to either ear. The descendant of an illustrious line of Catholic leaders, King Victor's dishonest intrigues were a continual disappointment to Pius IX. When the Pope rebuked him the king would apologize, beg forgiveness, promise to be good, and then betray Pius again.

When Victor sent the Brazilian Emperor to persuade
Pius to bury the hatchet, the pope replied: "If Your Majesty
brings Victor Emmanuel to me, I will speak to him with such
force that when he goes out of my study he'll be too stunned
to find the stairs."[1] Nevertheless, Pius and Victor continued
a correspondence through the saintly Piedmont priest Don
Bosco — the only man trusted by both.

After the fall of Rome, the city became the secular capital
of the new Kingdom of Italy. Victor Emmanuel moved into
the Quirinal Palace, the home of popes for centuries. The
king remained a foreigner in his own capital, a fact even the
secular press admitted:

> Italy is as much a stranger here as it was the first
> day. Rome does not resemble a friendly city, but
> a city constantly writhing under a prolonged mil-
> itary occupation which it bears impatiently.[2]

Victor Emmanuel never felt at home either, particularly
in his new residence in the Quirinal Palace, the centuries
long home of popes and saints:

> It was a palace which he had always feared to
> occupy, the very traditions of his house making it
> painful to him to have daily and hourly reminders
> of his spoliation of the Holy See before his eyes.
> He had avoided, as far as possible, sleeping even
> for one night in the plundered Pontifical palace.[3]

In the fall of 1877 Pius IX was ill and languishing in bed.
Many thought it was the end — including King Victor. He
began plans to influence the anticipated conclave to ensure
the election of a "liberal pope." Victor also completed a
decree regulating the funeral ceremonies and public mourning for the expected death of eighty-six-year-old Pius IX.

Twenty-five years the pope's junior, Victor's iron

---

[1] Thornton, *Cross Upon Cross*, 242
[2] Shea, *The Life of Pope Pius IX*, 381.
[3] O'Clery, *The Making of Italy*, 544.

constitution assured him a long reign as constitutional monarch — until he surprisingly contracted malaria in January 1878. The king pleaded to be taken from Rome, but his doctors forbade this. When Pius IX heard Victor was dying, he sent his own chaplain to the Quirinal to perform last rites.

The chaplain was refused entry. Pius persisted. "Deeply wronged as he was, the Pontiff thought only of soothing the passage to eternity of his chief despoiler."[4] To this end, Pius removed his many excommunications and again sent his chaplain to King Victor's bedside. He was finally allowed entry. In his last moments of life, Victor was reconciled to the Church and given last rites. He died on Jan 9, 1878 — a month before Pius himself died.

NAPOLEON III

After being routed by Prussia, Prince Louis Napoleon Bonaparte III lived in exile in England. He was plotting a return to power when his doctor discovered a kidney stone "as large as a walnut." On January 9, 1873, several attempts were made to crush the stone. The result was the patient expiring instead of the stone. A few minutes before his death, Napoleon received *Viaticum*.

Another medical mishap occurred during the embalming, which turned the Emperor's face bright yellow. By contrast, the doctors' faces were bright red, as the medical procedure Napoleon underwent was not considered a dangerous one.[5]

The European press lamented his death and cited Napoleon III's role in the *Risorgimento* as one of his main achievements. In fact, Napoleon's Italian policy — aiding Italy's *Risorgimento* while simultaneously protecting Rome from the *Risorgimento* with French troops — was muddled enough

---

[4] Ibid.
[5] Fenton Bresler, *Napoleon III, A Life* (New York: Carroll & Graf Publishers, Inc., 1999), 406–409. Napoleon III had a Catholic funeral at St. Mary's church near Chislehurst, England.

to anger everyone, even provoking several assassination attempts by disgruntled Freemasons like Orsini.

Msgr. George Dillon claimed the frequent assassination attempts made by Italian extremists against Napoleon aimed "to terrify him so that he as a *Carbonari* may be made to do its [Masonry's] work soon and effectively."[6] Napoleon III's most recent (secular) biographer concurs, quoting a close friend of Napoleon's:

> Louis Napoleon is determined to go to war with Austria to propitiate the Italians and to save his own life from assassination...Cavour worked upon this at their interview at Plombières and persuaded him that taking up the cause of Italy will save his life, forfeited according to the laws of the *Carbonari* (Napoleon's old Masonic order).[7]

There were other self-interests. Napoleon believed a unified Italy would be a stronger ally against Austria and Prussia. The fishbone in his throat was Pius IX and the Papal States — and later, the duplicity of Italy in not aiding him against Prussia.

GIUSEPPE MAZZINI

Napoleon's submission to the pressures of international Masonry neutralized the power of France to defend Pius IX from the Revolution. Yet even in victory, the Revolution's champions were dissatisfied.

Morose upon realizing most Italians cared for his revolution only to the extent it advanced their personal ambitions, arch-conspirator Giuseppe Mazzini lamented: "I had thought to evoke the soul of Italy, but all I find before me is its corpse."[8]

---

[6] A younger Napoleon joined the *Carbonari,* a Masonic Italian secret society instrumental in organizing the *Risorgimento.* Dillon, *Grand Orient Freemasonry Unmasked,* 91.

[7] The words of British Foreign Secretary Lord Malmesbury, a personal friend of Napoleon, as quoted in Bresler, *Napoleon III,* 294.

[8] Smith, *Italy: A Modern History,* 14

Mazzini did have a way with words. His triumphs were founding *Young Italy* and his short-lived leadership of the 1849 revolutionary government in Rome. Yet his high-sounding rhetoric — "Neither pope nor king, only God and the people will open the way of the future to us" — proved more style than substance.

A recent historian observes:

> In pursuing his goals, Mazzini developed an extremism of his own characterized by moral intransigence and faith in the superiority of spirit over matter... it was a highly individual religion that conformed to no established theology or norms... his talents were essentially those of the publicist. The appeal to conscience, the cult of martyrs, and the cultivation of an image of victim were part of his highly personal recipe for power.[9]

After being bounced out of Rome, Mazzini was condemned by Karl Marx for the unforgivable sin of putting religion ahead of the revolution. That overstated things, but no one ever accused Marx of being fair.

Mazzini fell out of favor permanently in Italy when he denounced the new kingdom formed by Cavour and Victor Emmanuel in 1861. By then, he had been rendered irrelevant by Cavour's war machine. Upon losing power, he disappeared.

Banned from France and Italy, Giuseppe Mazzini used an assumed name to sneak from Switzerland to Italy just in time to die of pleurisy in Pisa on March 10, 1872. His dying words were: "Yes, Yes, I believe in God..."[10]

Dying "an unhappy and disillusioned fugitive,"[11] he was honored by a public funeral and given a brutal obituary

[9] Roland Sarti, *Mazzini: A Life for the Religion of Politics* (Westport, CT: Greenwood Publishing Group, 1997), 178.
[10] Dennis Mack Smith, *Mazzini* (New Haven, CT: Yale University Press, 1994), 224.
[11] Smith, *Italy: A Modern History*, op. cit., p. 14.

by French Freemason Proudhon: "In his entire life Mazzini knew how to effect only two things; to draw money
from the rich and blood from the people. And he never
restored either."[12]

GIUSEPPE GARIBALDI

Although Garibaldi pointedly missed attending Mazzini's
funeral, he often spoke of Mazzini, for it was he whom
Garibaldi blamed for his military defeats at Rome, Mentana, and elsewhere.[13]

To his credit, Garibaldi admitted his greatest victory —
the conquest of Naples — would have been impossible without English money, soldiers, and ships.[14] Given his per-
petual outrage at the interference of foreigners in Italian
affairs, this is a curious admission; but no one ever claimed
Giuseppe Garibaldi was any less a hypocrite than his revolutionary companions.

Toward the end of his life, amidst mutterings about
"wolves and assassins" (i.e., the clergy), Garibaldi came
to the same bitter conclusions about Italy as Mazzini: the
Risorgimento was a fiction foisted on Italians who never
wanted unification and acted accordingly.[15] His obsessive
hatred of the Church intensified — if possible — in his retire-
ment on the island of Caprera.

Priests were "murderers of liberty," and the Papacy was
"the negation of God."[16] The only chief enemy to out-
live Pius IX, Garibaldi died on Caprera in 1882. His will
instructed that he be burned — not cremated — on a pyre,

---

[12] Rev. Reuben Parsons, *Studies in Church History*, 3rd ed. (Philadelphia:
John Joseph McVey, 1909), 5:537. Like the *Risorgimento*, Mazzini grows
more popular the hazier history gets, which may explain why Proudhon
ended his obituary: "Truly the Italians are patient."
[13] Mazzini was guilty of many things, but he was not responsible for
Garibaldi's military defeats.
[14] Courtesy of high-ranking Freemason Lord Palmerston. See Parsons,
Studies in Church History, 5:533–534, and Dillon, *Grand Orient Freemasonry Unmasked*, chap. 17., (entitled Lord Palmerston).
[15] Smith, *Italy: A Modern History*, 81–82, 89.
[16] Martin, *The Red Shirt and the Cross of Savoy*, 732.

adding: "You will need plenty of wood." The Italian government thwarted Garibaldi one last time and buried him in a coffin instead.

His funeral was less public than Mazzini's but more dramatic. According to Garibaldi's secular biographer:

> When his body was lowered into the earth, the sky darkened, a strong wind sprang up, and in a flash the heavens opened and rain poured down; at the same moment the block of granite which was to be laid over his grave cracked and broke.[17]

---

[17] Ibid.

. . . .

CHAPTER 29

"PRISONER OF THE VATICAN"

GARIBALDI and Mazzini were honest enough to admit then what can be openly admitted today: the *Risorgimento* was not a popular uprising of downtrodden masses seizing freedom from tyranny. It was instead a series of violent attacks plotted by a few men bent on breaking the temporal power of the Church and, if possible, destroying the papacy. Once power was seized the cat leapt out of the bag.

"The revolutionary attempts which have occurred since 1821 in Italy were the work of Freemasonry," declared a high-ranking French Freemason.[1] An author present in Italy during the *Risorgimento* wrote:

> There is but a scanty basis for the legend that represents the revolution that began in 1856 and ended in 1870 as anything like the act of the Italian people as a whole. It was the act of a party, accomplished throughout by the help of foreign arms, in the interest of a section of the people, and against the armed protest of whole districts of the country. To put it...in its true light is to take away from it that halo of consecration as a national movement...it has no right to any such title.[2]

Pio Nono was right: the Church was the target of the Revolution, who used the *Risorgimento* as a battering ram. "The destruction of the temporal power of the papacy was the climax of the *Risorgimento* and perhaps

---

[1] Leon de Poncins, *The Secret Powers Behind Revolution*, repr. (Colton, Calif.: Christian Book Club, 1986), 65–65.
[2] O'Clery, The Making of Italy, 551.

its most important achievement," according to the leading English-speaking historian on modern Italy.[3] In due course, Ernesto Nathan — identified by the same secular historian as "the grand master of Italian Freemasonry," — became mayor of Rome.[4]

PRISONER OF THE VATICAN

According to Henri Daniel-Rops, during the final years of Pius IX's life:

> Strongly anti-clerical elements were managing the affairs of Italy; within eighteen months thirty-two religious communities had been dispossessed in Rome; the faculties of theology were abolished in the universities; and Freemasons were taking charge in high places.[5]

A Protestant church appeared in Rome — and then a Masonic temple.[6] The prophecy of Anna Maria Taigi, made prior to Pius' pontificate, seemed to have come to pass: "the Pope, shut up in the Vatican, would find himself hemmed in as by an iron circle."[7]

The fact that it was not safe to walk the streets of Rome in religious dress added a literal dimension to Pius IX's position as "Prisoner of the Vatican." So did the rifles trained on Vatican windows to discourage direct appeals to crowds.[8]

Those who fault Pio Nono for melodrama in "styling" himself a prisoner fail to account for these realities — or for the fact that Pius' successors vigorously adopted Pius' uncompromising protests. His successor, the "liberal" Pope Leo XIII, "protested over sixty times, and on at least four occasions allowed a rumor to spread that he might remove

---

[3] Smith, *Italy: A Modern History*, 96.
[4] Ibid., 226. The English born Nathan was mayor from 1907–1913.
[5] Daniel-Rops, *The Church in an Age of Revolution*, 303.
[6] Smith, *Italy: A Modern History*, 98.
[7] Thompson, *The Life of the Venerable Anna Maria Taigi, The Roman Matron*, 321.
[8] Shea, *The Life of Pope Pius IX*, 357.

from Rome to a new Avignon. Up to 1929 this formal protest was maintained and the very suggestion of compromise
repudiated."[9]

It was not until the pontificate of Pius XI that territory
was given back to the Church and popes stopped protesting
the seizure of Rome.

PIO MARIA MORTARA

After Rome fell, Mortara was pressured to give up his religious vocation and return to his family. "The police followed
my every step," he recalled, "and every night they placed
guards near the convent to prevent an escape."

Pius inquired anxiously about Edgardo's welfare. Perhaps he was involved with Edgardo's quiet escape from
Rome; after all, Pio Nono himself had once disappeared
from Rome despite being heavily guarded. Pius' reaction to
Edgardo's departure was: "We thank the Lord that Mortara
has escaped."[10]

He and Pius never saw each other again but the Pope kept
in touch with Edgardo and his superiors — first in Austria
and then in France, where Mortara was placed under the
watchful eye of Cardinal Pie of Poitiers. In 1873 Edgardo
was ordained a priest.

> "On the happy day of my first Mass," he recalled,
> Pius IX "honored me with a personally signed
> letter, which I retain as a precious relic.... He
> asked me to pray especially for him and to act to
> the limits of my strength for the glory of God and
> the good of souls."[11]

For the next sixty-seven years, Father Pio Maria Mortara "dedicated his life to spreading the faith, singing the

---

[9] Smith, *Italy: A Modern History*, 98.
[10] Mortara's beatification testimony, secs. 1665 and 1664, respectively.
Like Pius IX, Edgardo escaped Rome with a companion, both of whom
were dressed in lay clothes.
[11] Ibid., sec. 1671. Pius also provided Mortara with a lifetime pension
from his private funds.

praises of the Lord Jesus Christ, and traveling throughout Europe, going where he was most needed." [12] He mas-
tered six languages and preached in them all, particularly
to Jewish audiences. A newspaper report of this time
described him:

> Of medium height, he is a man with a most pleas-
> ing appearance, with a gentle and courteous man-
> ner, and an entirely Christian kindness about him.
> His modesty, his simplicity moved us, knowing
> that his learning and his fame are known through-
> out the world....We were extremely pleased to
> have heard him. We blessed God, who in the
> inscrutable ways of his providence, permitted
> the acquisition to Catholicism of such a powerful
> champion of the faith. [13]

Father Mortara traveled around the world, including a
trip to New York to establish missions for Italian immigrants.
He acquired a reputation in the Church as a "saintly, pious,
tireless worker," whose "sermons breathed fire and passion,
despite his frail health." [14] He spoke often of his conversion,
never failing to give heartfelt thanks to Blessed Pius IX.
Recalling how Pius would greet him with a smile and the
words, "At your service, Mortara," Pio Maria declared: "And
it was really a true service that was done for me by that man,
who officially called himself '*Servus servorum Dei*.'" [15]

After the First World War Father Mortara joined an abbey
in Bouhay, Belgium "dedicated to contemplation, study,

---

[12] Kertzer, *The Kidnapping of Edgardo Mortara*, 295.

[13] This particular incident occurred at Modena, Italy, the birthplace
of Edgardo's mother. Several of Edgardo's brothers and sisters were
in attendance. Edgardo had been at his mother's deathbed the previous year, trying as always to convert her. He was unsuccessful (Ibid.,
296–297).

[14] Korn, *American Reaction to the Mortara Case, 1858–1859*, 160.

[15] "Servant of the servants of God." See Mortara's beatification testimony, sec. 1661. Later this title of Pius IX was borrowed by a post-
conciliar pope. This title was first used by Pope Saint Gregory the
Great (590–604).

prayer, and devotion to the Virgin Mary, for whom he had a special fondness."[16] According to David Kertzer,

> Bouhay was renowned for its sanctuary to the Virgin of Lourdes...and Pio Edgardo felt a special, spiritual link to the miracle at Lourdes. The Virgin had chosen to reveal herself to the faithful in 1858, and so two miracles took place in the same year, one in a French town, the other in Italy, when the Virgin appeared to a little boy just plucked from his Jewish home, a boy who, in a few days' time, went from the obscurity of life as the sixth child of a modest merchant's family to the heights of celebrity...[17]

Like fellow Jewish converts Father Marie Alphonse and Father Théodore Marie Ratisbonne, Father Pio Maria Mortara died a peaceful death in the Belgian abbey on March 11, 1940, just before the Nazis invaded Belgium.

---

[16] Kertzer, *The Kidnapping of Edgardo Mortara*, 297–298.
[17] Ibid., 297–298. This is moving prose from a secular Jewish historian. At the risk of spoiling it, I am unaware of the Virgin's appearance to little Edgardo implied by Professor Kertzer.

CHAPTER 30

. . . .

BEATIFICATION

FTER Mortara's death the canonization cause of
Pius IX stalled. Kenneth L. Woodward, *Newsweek's*
religion editor and author of *Making Saints,*[1] says
the delay was due to Pius' Devil Advocate[2] making the same
objections the Church's enemies made against Pius during
his pontificate.

THE "DEVIL'S ADVOCATE"

So we find Pio Nono faulted again for "lacking prudence
in government;"—that is, for not being friendly enough
to the Revolution. According to Woodward, Pope Paul VI
wondered why Pius IX didn't follow the advice of Antonio
Rosmini who urged Pius to "baptize" the *Risorgimento* and
the "principles of '89."[3]

Was Pope Paul truly unaware of the famous case where
Father Félicité Lammenais baptized the Revolution and then
apostatized?

Some consultors to Pius' canonization cause accused him
of "a serious lack of charity toward neighbor." The charge is
unspecific, but one suspects the neighbors in question were
liberals, Freemasons, and revolutionaries—not the poor,

---

[1] Subtitled *How the Catholic Church Determines Who Becomes a Saint, Who
Doesn't, and Why* (New York: Touchstone Books, 1996)
[2] A nickname for the Promoter of the Faith, a Church official who
challenges the advocates of a proposed saint to test the merits of their
cause. The office was created in the fourteenth century as part of a
reform of the canonization process.
[3] Hales, *Pio Nono*, 84. Rosmini was a liberal and his sympathizers, which
have included Popes John XXIII and Paul VI, support his canonization.
Rosmini's current supporters are miffed Pius IX ignored Rosmini's
advice and never made him a cardinal. Worse, during Pius' pontificate
the Holy Office condemned some of Rosmini's writings for promoting
pantheism (see Daniel-Rops, *The Church in an Age of Revolution*, 318).

cholera victims, injured Jews, orphaned boys, and innumerable others on whom Pius repeatedly bestowed quiet, heartfelt charity.[4]

This alleged lack of charity perhaps includes Pius' refusal to commute the death sentences of Monti and Tognetti, two Garibaldian Freemasons[5] who blew up a barracks in Rome, killing two dozen papal Zouaves and badly wounding many others. At the time (1867), Pius' decision "elicited a howl of rage from the revolutionary press"—not at the cold-blooded murder of two dozen men, but at the punishment given the two murderers.

The English press was very critical of the Pope's decision. In response, Pius noted the British government's brutal suppression of an insurrection in Jamaica where hundreds were killed, and remarked:

> When, to my very great regret and my profound grief, I am constrained to permit a criminal to be executed in my States, from all sides are raised the most frightful clamours. I am "a tyrant!" "an executioner!" "a King eager to shed blood!" But when your Government summarily destroys some hundreds of negroes [sic)]...it is a simple act of justice.[6]

The Devil's Advocate also accused Pius IX of cowardice for escaping the Roman Revolution in 1848, a charge even one of Pius' critics refused to hurl. The critic, Adolphus Trollope, spent two volumes criticizing Pio Nono for innumerable transgressions, yet understood why Pius left Rome. He stated the Pope could not

> ...in any degree be blamed for having come to such a resolution (to leave Rome)...the desires

---

[4] See Woodward, *Making Saints*, 315.
[5] Ibid., 315–316. Woodward has the date wrong; it was 1867, not 1862. For some reason he refers to Monti and Tognetti as "anarchists," perhaps because bombs were common weapons for anarchists. They were in fact Freemasons on assignment from Garibaldi.
[6] Maguire, *Pontificate of Pius the Ninth*, 458.

of the mob "were absolutely and fundamentally incompatible with the existence of a Pope King, if not with that of any king at all.

In fact it was neither pragmatism nor cowardice that decided things for Pius. Rather, he believed he received a sign from Heaven to leave Rome when he was given a small silver container in which another papal exile, Pius VII, had carried the Blessed Sacrament.[7]

Pio Nono was further faulted for issuing the *Syllabus of Errors* (it was "inopportune") and for not allowing freer discussion on papal infallibility during the Council. This is simply unhistorical (see Chapter 14).

Last, Pius was blamed for,

A number of harmful effects to the Church: notably, the "violent" [sic] loss of the Papal States, the "more violent" [sic] continuing conflict between church and state in Italy, including "unrestrained anticlericalism."[8]

It is curious logic indeed to blame a ruler not just for defending himself against an aggressive invasion but also for the frenzied excesses of the invaders as well.

Unfortunately, the criticisms of the Devil's Advocate are mere calumny — particularly the charge that Pius failed in charity. Even Pio Nono's opponents concede his large heartedness. "Tell Garibaldi that this poor old man whom he calls the vampire of the Vatican forgives him, prays for him, and this very morning said Mass for him," Pius informed an acquaintance familiar with both men.[9] Professor Toli said of Pius IX, "It will be easier to count the paving stones in Rome than to count the examples of his charity."[10]

---

[7] T. Adolphus Trollope, *The Story of the Life of Pius The Ninth*, vol. 1 (London: Richard Bentley and Son, 1877), 295–297.
[8] Woodward, *Making Saints*, 317.
[9] *CRC* September 2000.
[10] Ibid.

The point here is not to criticize the Devil's Advocate (more properly called the Promoter of the Faith). It is a worthy office that for centuries has protected the faith by testing the mettle of canonization causes. Rather, it is to observe that the Devil's Advocate in Pio Nono's cause does not protect the Catholic faith; it protects faith in the Revolution.

Misuse of the Devil's Advocate office may perhaps be traced back to the Second Vatican Council.[11] Since the Council, Pius' canonization was twice stalled by Vatican judges,[12] once by a secret commission,[13] and once by his Italian biographer, the Jesuit Martina.[14]

Given that much of the contemporary Vatican hierarchy has accepted the liberal/Masonic view of Pio Nono, his beatification—while falling short of miraculous—was certainly highly improbable. It is reminiscent of the canonization of Father Kolbe which, although done for the wrong reasons, still raised before the world another truly Marian saint.

THE ANTI-COUNCIL OF NAPLES

The double beatification of Pio Nono and "Good Pope John" in 2000 is a bit of a head-scratcher. Are there similarities between the two men? Well, both were Italian popes who convoked councils, and both were accused of liberalism and Freemasonry.[15] After this—the abyss. Like

---

[11] One thing Pius was not reproached for was an alleged anti-Semitic comment he made about the "dogs of Rome," a supposed allusion to Rome's Jews. It is very surprising this was not raised during Pius' canonization. David Kertzer never mentioned it either, nor is it mentioned in any of the many biographies and other books on Pius IX I used in researching this series. According to *America* (Sept. 16, 2000), the remarks, which were intended as an analogy about the children of God, were made in a speech given by Pius in 1871. I have never seen it mentioned anywhere else.

[12] *Newsweek,* September 4, 2000.

[13] Ibid.

[14] *America,* September 16, 2000.

[15] Some view Pio Nono as a reformed Freemason, or at least an ex-liberal. Do we really want to give credit for all of Pio Nono's early reforms,

virtually all his predecessors, Pio Nono felt duty-bound to defend the Church, at times via formal condemnations.

By contrast, the only thing Pope John condemned was condemnations. This made him "good" in the world's eyes, but in fact rendered his council morally suspect for failing to condemn — or even mention — the Communism of its day, which was murderous indeed.

It is said Pope John desired the beatification of Pius IX. Perhaps he did, although surely he considered Pius IX one of those "prophets of gloom" who see "only ruin and calamity in modern times."[16] Good Pope John opened the Second Vatican Council with this rebuke, then proclaimed a "new order of human relations" requiring "use of the medicine of mercy rather than that of severity."[17] Many decades later we still await this new order, which we are assured is ever aborning.

Pius IX opened the First Vatican Council by rebuking "a conspiracy of the wicked, mighty by combination, rich in resources, fortified with institutions, and using liberty for a cloak of maliciousness."[18] An *enemy* of Pio Nono described what happened next:

> As the Pontiff drew to the close of his allocu-
> tion, he, with a burst of feeling, put up two
> invocations, one to the Holy Spirit, the other to

a number of which were good, to "liberalism"? I don't. Neither does Garibaldi's biographer, George Martin, who notes that the Revolution itself "misunderstood" Pius, who "conceived of the Papal government, spiritual and temporal, as a trust committed to him personally, which he was to discharge personally. He could be liberal *in the exercise of his authority*, which he had tried to be in 1848, but he could not introduce liberal institutions into his government...for they presupposed a sharing of his personal authority." (Martin, *The Red Shirt and the Cross of Savoy*, 592–593, my emphasis).

[16] Walter M. Abbott, S. J., ed., *The Documents of Vatican II* (New York: Guild Press, 1966), 712, and Romano Amerio, *Iota Unum: A Study of Changes in the Catholic Church in the 20th Century* (Kansas City, MO: Sarto House, 1996), 74.

[17] Abbott, *The Documents of Vatican II*, 712, 716.

[18] Rev. William Arthur, *The Pope, the Kings, and the People* (London: Hodder and Stoughton, 1903), 295–296.

> the Blessed Virgin. After this, with contagious
> intensity of emotion, he threw up both hands to
> heaven. At a bound, the whole assembly stood
> up. Then he poured forth the final invocation
> with the fullest resonance of his wonderful
> tones...
>
> He invoked angels and archangels, Peter,
> Paul, and all the saints, more particularly those
> whose ashes were venerated on that spot. This
> speech from the apostolic throne... beginning
> with the liveliest joy, afterwards expressing
> divine agonies, concluded with firm and tran-
> quil confidence![19]

Speaking of enemies of Pio Nono — on that same day,
December 8, 1869 — a group of Freemasons began an anti-
Council at Naples to "recognise and proclaim liberty of
conscience, freedom of enquiry [sic]), and the dignity of
man." Due to the violence and ferocity of these meetings,
the anti-Council was forced to change locations from a
theater to a hotel. Eventually they were all arrested,[20]
but not before calling for "the rejection of every dogma
founded upon revelation," and declaring:

> Whereas the idea of God is the source and the
> support of every despotism and of every iniq-
> uity; whereas the Catholic religion is the most
> complete and the most terrible personifica-
> tion of this idea, the sum of its dogmas being
> the negation of society — the Free-Thinkers of
> Paris assume as an obligation to abolish Cath-
> olicity promptly and radically, and to employ
> for its *annihilation* all means compatible with
> justice, comprehending within these means

---

[19] Ibid., 296. According to Msgr. Guerin. Rev. Arthur's book is subtitled *"A History of the Movement to make the Pope Governor of the World
by a Universal Reconstruction of Society from the Issue of the Syllabus to the
Close of the Vatican Council."* Can't wait for the movie.
[20] Maguire, *The Pontificate of Pius the Ninth*, 536–538.

revolutionary force, the which is but the applica-
tion to society of the right of *legitimate defence*.[21]

The key word here is "annihilation." As previously
noted, "legitimate defense" has included invading peaceful areas to kill thousands of innocent people, and to loot,
pillage, and steal property both real and personal. All in
the name of "legitimate defense." Euphemisms are handy
tools, no?

---

[21] Ibid., 537. Emphasis supplied.

CHAPTER 31

THE BELOVED

LTHOUGH the differences between Pius IX and John XXIII are not as deep as the differences between the Vatican Council and the Masonic anti-Council of Naples, it suspends reality to claim these two popes have anything but superficialities in common. Liberals recognize this as well, as evidenced by a *Commonweal* editorial prior to the double beatification:

> So why a Blessed Pio Nono now?...The pope of Vatican II cannot be promoted without match-ing him with the pope of Vatican I. The idea that Vatican II and all it represents is not just a development of Vatican I and all it represents, but is, in important respects, a corrective, is unpalatable in present-day Rome...The splen-did absurdity of the coming event can be grasped when we recognize that John XXIII and John Paul II would both have been condemned for their ideas and their words had they expressed them when Pius IX was in power...[1]

A TALE OF TWO COUNCILS

Yes, they probably would have — although another "splendid absurdity" *Commonweal* may not wish to ponder is a comparison of the fruits of Pio Nono's Council with those of Pope John's.[2] Even though abbreviated, the First

---

[1] *Commonweal*, August 11, 2000. *Inside The Vatican* (August/September 2000, 75) maintained politics had nothing to do with John Paul II's decision to beatify Pio Nono and John XXIII together. There was talk that Pius XII was supposed to be Pope John's beatification partner, but the flap over Pius' alleged anti-Semitism — which is denied even by many prominent Jews — apparently made him too controversial, and he was replaced by the "non-controversial" Pio Nono.

[2] Pius IX left the Church stronger than when he found it. As for

Vatican Council strengthened the Church. The Second Vatican Council began an unraveling process that continues today. While a pope cannot be held accountable for all the (often unforeseen) results of a council, it can be argued that each Vatican Council bore the mark of the pope who convened it—and the fruits thereof.

Over a century ago, Blessed Pius IX spoke of "that fatal system which is always dreaming of accommodating two irreconcilable things, the Church and the Revolution. I have already condemned this, but I would condemn it again forty times if necessary... it is this game of seesaw which will end up destroying religion."[3] He was referring to Catholic liberalism, which he called a "true plague."[4] He believed the downfall of liberal Catholics, including Montalembert, was pride: "Liberal Catholics are half-Catholics," he concluded.[5]

John XXIII was the pope of the revolution, and Pius IX was pope of the counter-revolution. And speaking of differences, unlike Pope John Paul II, Pius IX actively discouraged attempts to name him "Great:"

> A deputation of Roman nobility saluted Pius IX as "Pius the Great" and offered him a throne of gold. Pius IX declined both title and throne with firmness, and yet with all his wonted cheerfulness: "What! In my lifetime! I admire your imprudence. The Church to canonize her saints waits till they are dead, and long dead. Humanity should be in no greater haste to canonize her

---

Pope John, let's just say there were very good reasons he had a short pontificate.

[3] *CRC*, September 2000.

[4] Once he said liberal Catholicism was worse than the Communists of Paris. See Mortara's beatification testimony, sec. 1676.

[5] Arthur, *The Pope, the Kings, and the People*, 485. Pius also spoke of some bishops at Vatican I who, "like Pilate when terrified by the Jews, are afraid to do right. They fear the Revolution. Though knowing the truth, they sacrifice all to Caesar, even the rights of the Holy See, and their attachment to the Vicar of Jesus Christ. Wretches! What a fault they commit!" (Ibid., 499).

heroes, for so long as a man breathes, no one
can aver that his heroism will not belie itself."[6]

"THE BELOVED"

True words indeed. But they do not describe Blessed
Pius IX who "to the very last retained all his pugnacity
and strength of soul ... All were struck by his charm, his
affability, the noble simplicity of his welcome and that
sense of humour which seldom deserted him even in his
darkest hour."[7]

Was he great? Sure. But as great as Pius was — as a
priest, a pope, a king, and a man — the word that fits him
best is: *beloved.*

"We find no one," Mgr. O'Reilly wrote of Pius' predecessors, "to whom the enthusiastic and disinterested love of
the Catholic world has paid such repeated, such unanimous,
and such splendid testimony of filial regard and unbounded
attachment"[8] as to Pius IX, of which a contemporary said:

> Never under any of the successors of Saint Peter
> has one seen Christian doctrines affirmed with
> more force or Catholic unity demonstrated in
> a more marvelous fashion. Despite the baseness
> and deficiencies of the present time, the civilized
> world has been able to contemplate ... an elderly
> man invested with the double character of Pontiff
> and King, inaccessible to fear no less than flattery,
> opposing brute force with a calm conscience and
> the holiness of justice, never bringing violence or
> lies to bear in any transaction ...
>
> ... and benefiting from each new insult to pro-
> claim once more, before the eyes of an indifferent
> or hostile world, the principles of truth and good,
> the invariable laws of morality, the maxims of
> equity and justice. An incomparable spectacle, well

---

[6] Shea, *The Life of Pope Pius IX* , 382.
[7] Daniel-Rops, *The Church in an Age of Revolution*, 302, 275–276.
[8] O'Reilly, *A Life of Pius IX*, 529.

calculated to comfort our hearts and to force the admiration of even our very adversaries.[9]

He laid his Father's hand on all the festering wounds of modern society, not to inflame them but to cleanse and dress them. For this he was buffeted and mocked. With spittle streaming down his face, he persevered with the courage of a lion, the humility of a martyr, and the holiness of a saint. He was:

> A character consummate in its perfection, a great man, greater than any other of the generation in which he lived, for no one consecrated so long a life as he to so grand an idea with such energy and wisdom; no one bore so loftily as he the standard of truth and justice on the cruel battle-ground of these evil days.[10]

An American priest wrote the following poem, entitled *After Seeing Pius IX:*

> I saw his face today; he looks like a chief
> Who fears not human rage, nor human guile;
> Upon his cheeks the twilight of a grief,
> But in that grief the starlight of a smile.
> Deep, gentle eyes, with drooping lids that tell
> They are the homes where tears of sorrow dwell;
>
> A low voice — strangely sweet — whose very tone
> Tells how these lips speak oft with God alone.
> I kissed His hand, I fain would kiss his feet;
> "No, no," he said; and then, in accents sweet,
> His blessing fell upon my bended head.
>
> He bade me rise; a few more words he said,
> Then took me by the hand — the while he smiled —
> And, going, whispered: "Pray for me, my child."[11]

---

[9] From an 1871 pastoral letter by Mgr. Greppel, quoted in *CRC*, September 2000.
[10] Rev. Constantine Kempf, S. J., *The Holiness of the Church in the Nineteenth Century, Saintly Men and Women of Our Own Times* (New York: Benziger Brothers, 1916), 33.
[11] Father Abram J. Ryan, *Poems: Patriotic, Religious, Miscellaneous* (New York: P. J. Kenedy & Sons, 1896).

His favorite prayer to the Blessed Virgin — "My Queen! My Mother! Remember I am thine own; Keep me, guard me, as thy property and possession" — led naturally to Pius' consecration of the Church to the Sacred Heart of Jesus.[12] His evident proximity to the Holy Hearts allowed him, after three decades of being battered and besieged, to calmly state: *Ipse vero dormiebat* — "Yet he slept well," a reference to Christ sleeping during the tempest.[13]

When admonished by a French diplomat on the needs of modern society, Pius courteously replied, "What you call modern society is simply Freemasonry."[14] And when threatened with violence if he did not return a young baptized Jew to his non-Christian parents, he replied that all the bayonets in the world would not make him abandon Edgardo Mortara.[15]

Father Mortara would have been proud of Pio Nono's beatification, but hardly surprised. "I have the almost instinctive conviction that one day he will be raised to the glory of the altars," he testified.[16] When in Rome he made a point to visit Pius' grave. There old memories came back, and as Mortara said, "[I] prostrated myself on the tomb of my august father and protector, toward whom my gratitude knows no limits, and whom I will always hold to be a wise and saintly Pontiff. In his epitaph he invites the faithful to pray for him: '*Orate pro eo.*' I confess that whenever I read those words, I said in my heart, '*Sancte Pie, ora pro me*'" — Saint Pius, pray for me.[17]

---

[12] In 1875. Pius also extended the Feast of the Sacred Heart to the Universal Church (1856) and beatified Margaret Mary Alacoque (August 19, 1864), giving formal approval to the apparitions of the Sacred Heart.

[13] Mortara's beatification testimony, sec. 1660. See also Matthew 8:23–27 and Luke 8:23–25.

[14] Kertzer, *The Kidnapping of Edgardo Mortara*, 157.

[15] Mortara's beatification testimony, sec. 1678

[16] Ibid., sec. 1695.

[17] Ibid., sec. 1672.

CHAPTER 32

ADDIO

IS final acts were reestablishing the Scottish hierarchy and appointing the first cardinals to the Church in America. Then the strong legs that had carried him on so many walks through Rome simply gave out, and Pius could no longer stand when celebrating Mass. After generously allowing the recently deceased King Victor to be buried in the Church of St. Mary of the Martyrs (commonly known as the Pantheon) Pius conducted business from bed.

At his bedside was Cardinal Manning: gaunt, grimly ascetic, and striving against himself to ensure "no business, however slight, was ever introduced. I felt that the sick-bed of Pius IX was sacred," Manning recalled. By contrast the Pope was his calm, cheerful, sympathetic self, no doubt appreciating the pains his friend took to adopt a bedside manner.

Perhaps they recalled the American bishop who interrupted Vatican Council debate to insist that clerics should not be allowed to hunt with guns, or the Council Father who thought all priests should be required to grow beards. On Wednesday Pius walked a few steps. That night he contracted a fever.

On Thursday morning, February 7, 1878, his pulse was rapid and weak. Pius greeted his doctor and smiled: "This time it's the end." *Viaticum* was administered. Manning rushed into the room and kissed the pope's hand. Pius smiled and whispered: "*Addio, carissimo.*" Goodbye, dearest one.

Other Cardinals gathered at his bed and began the *Proficiscere* prayer: "Go forth Christian soul," to which Pius fervently responded "Yes, go forth." These were his last words. The final act of his life was to bless the cardinals with that long ago gift from his mother—his trusty lemonwood crucifix.

That afternoon he lost consciousness. His breathing was labored. He clutched his crucifix as, one by one, the crosses were lifted from him. His breathing slowed as the cardinals began reciting the Sorrowful Mysteries. The bells of St. Peter's pealed the evening Angelus, known in Italy as the *Ave Maria*. He died as the bells rang.

Perhaps the bells that rang announced not only the death of Blessed Pope Pius IX, but also the hour of his Visitation. Was the single tear that lay on his cheek evidence that the Immaculate had come again, this time to take her beloved son home?

The Prisoner of the Vatican was free at last.

A POPULAR contemporary expression is "You're history." The implication is that the one who is "history" will either be killed or has been rendered irrelevant or insignificant.

In some ways, however, we *are* history, and intelligent people have always known this — be they Church Fathers or Freemasons.

One of the earliest traditions of the pre-Christian Church kept vivid the memory of past heroes of the faith. This tradition shines forth in *Ecclesiasticus* (also known as *Sirach*), and is fitting for the last Pope-King, Blessed Pius IX:

> *Let us now praise famous men, and our*
> *fathers in their generations.*
> *The Lord apportioned to them great glory...*
> *Those who ruled in their kingdoms, and*
> *were men renowned for their power,*
> *giving counsel by their understanding...*
> *wise in their words of instruction.*
> *There are some of them who have left a name,*
> *so that men declare their praise.*
> *And there are some who have no memorial,*
> *who have perished as though they had not lived;*
> *they have become as though they had not been born...*
> *But these were men of mercy,*
> *whose righteous deeds have not been forgotten;*
> *their prosperity will remain with their descendants...*
> *and their glory will not be blotted out.*
> *Let the people show forth their wisdom,*
> *and the Church declare their praise.*

Let us now praise famous men.

BIBLIOGRAPHY

Abbott, Walter M., S.J., ed. *The Documents of Vatican II*. New York: Guild Press, 1966.

Aladel, M., C.M. *The Miraculous Medal: Its Origin, History, Circulation, Results*. Translated from the French. Boonville, N.Y.: Preserving Christian Publications, 1999.

Amerio, Romano. *Iota Unum: A Study of Changes in the Catholic Church in the Twentieth Century*. Kansas City, Mo.: Sarto House, 1996.

Arthur, Rev. William. *The Pope, the Kings, and the People*. London: Hodder and Stoughton, 1903.

Bernadette of Lourdes. *Bernadette of Lourdes*. Translated by J. H. Gregory. Nevers, France: St. Gildard, 1926.

Bessières, Albert, S.J. *Wife, Mother and Mystic (Blessed Anna-Maria Taigi)*. Translated by Rev. Stephen Rigby. Westminster, Md.: Newman Press, 1952.

Bokenkotter, Thomas. *A Concise History of the Catholic Church*. New York: Image Books Doubleday, 1990.

Brennan, Rev. Richard. *Life of Pope Pius IX*. New York: Benziger Brothers, 1878.

Bresler, Fenton. *Napoleon III: A Life*. New York: Carroll & Graf Publishers, 1999.

Browne-Olf, Lillian. *Their Name Is Pius*. Milwaukee: Bruce Publishing Company, 1941.

Cahill, Rev. E., S.J. *Freemasonry and the Anti-Christian Movement*. Dublin: M. H. Gill and Son, 1949.

Conversion of Ratisbonne: Narratives of Alphonse Ratisbonne and Baron Theodore de Bussieres. Harrison, N.Y.: Roman Catholic Books, 2000.

Corti, Count Egon. *The Reign of the House of Rothschild*. Translated by Brian and Beatrix Lunn. London: Victor Gollancz, 1928.

Daniel-Rops, Henri. *The Church in an Age of Revolution, 1789–1870*. New York: E. P. Dutton & Co., 1965.

Dewar, Diana. *The Saint of Auschwitz: The Story of Maximilian Kolbe*. New York: Harper & Row, 1982.

Dillon, Mgr. George E., D.D. *Grand Orient Freemasonry Unmasked*. Originally published 1885. Reprint, Hawthorne, Calif.: Christian Book Club. See Chapter 10, "Napoleon and Freemasonry."

Dirvin, Father Joseph I., C.M. *Saint Catherine Labouré of the Miraculous Medal*. Reprint, Rockford, Ill.: TAN Books and Publishers, 1984.

Elliot, Frances Minto. *Roman Gossip.* Leipzig: Tauchnitz, 1896.

Estrade, J. B. *My Witness, Bernadette: The Authentic Source Book of the Apparitions at Lourdes by an Eyewitness.* Reprint, Dublin: Cahill & Co., 1951.

Fahey, Rev. Denis. *The Mystical Body of Christ and the Reorganization of Society.* Cork: The Forum Press, 1945.

Fathers of La Salette. *La Salette.* Hartford, Conn.: Published by the Fathers of La Salette, 1901.

Fellows, Mark. *The Ninth Pius: The Last Pope-King.* Minneapolis, Minn.: Remnant Press, 1996.

Gouin, Fr. Paul. *Sister Mary of the Cross, Shepherdess of La Salette.* New Jersey: 101 Foundation, n.d.

Gray, Robert. *Cardinal Manning.* London: Weidenfeld & Nicolson, 1985.

Hales, E. E. Y. *Pio Nono: Creator of the Modern Papacy.* New York: P. J. Kenedy & Sons, 1954.

Halperin, William. *Italy and the Vatican at War.* Chicago: University of Chicago Press, 1939.

Hayes, Carlton J. H. *The Historical Evolution of Modern Nationalism.* New York: Richard R. Smith, Inc., 1931.

Ineffabilis Deus: Defining the Dogma of the Immaculate Conception. Apostolic Constitution of Pius IX, issued 1854. Reprint, Boston: St. Paul Books and Media, n.d.

Kempf, Rev. Constantine, S.J. *The Holiness of the Church in the Nineteenth Century: Saintly Men and Women of Our Own Times.* New York: Benziger Brothers, 1916.

Kertzer, David I. *The Kidnapping of Edgardo Mortara.* New York: Alfred A. Knopf, 1997.

Korn, Bertram. *American Reaction to the Mortara Case, 1858–1859.* Cincinnati: American Jewish Archives, 1957.

Maguire, John Francis, M.P. *Pontificate of Pius the Ninth.* London: Longmans, Green, and Co., 1870.

Manning, Henry Edward. *The True Story of the Vatican Council.* London: Burns & Oates, 1877.

Martin, George. *The Red Shirt and the Cross of Savoy: The Story of Italy's Risorgimento (1748–1871).* New York: Dodd, Mead & Company, 1969.

Mirari Vos. Encyclical by Pope Gregory XVI, issued August 1832. Reprint, Kansas City, Mo.: Angelus Press, 1998.

Montfort, St. Louis de. *True Devotion to Mary.* Rockford, Ill.: TAN Books and Publishers, 1985.

Metternich, Prince Richard, ed. *Memoirs of Prince Metternich, 1815–1829.* Vol. 3. New York: Howard Fertig, 1970. Photo reprint of Charles Scribner's Sons 1881 edition. Presented electronically by Paul Halsall in the Internet Modern History Sourcebook.

Nineteenth Century Miracle: The Brothers Ratisbonne and the Congregation of Notre Dame des Sion. Translated by L. M. Leggatt. London: Burns Oates & Washbourne, n.d.

Norwich, John Julius. *The Middle Sea: A History of the Mediterranean.* New York: Vintage Books, 2006.

O'Clery, Patrick Keyes. *The Making of Italy.* London: Kegan Paul, Trench, Trubner & Co., 1892.

O'Reilly, Rev. Bernard. *The Life of Pope Leo XIII, From His Personal Memoirs.* Philadelphia: John C. Winston Company, 1903.

———. *The Life of Pope Pius IX.* New York: P. F. Collier, 1877.

Parsons, Rev. Reuben. *Studies in Church History.* 3rd ed. Philadelphia: John Joseph McVey, 1909.

Poncins, Léon de. *The Secret Powers Behind Revolution.* Reprint, Hawthorne, Calif.: Christian Book Club, 1986.

Positio super Introductione Causae. Testimony for the beatification of Pope Pius IX by Father Pio Maria Mortara (formerly Edgardo Levi-Mortara), from the original Italian edition published in 1954. Translated and presented electronically by Zenit, September 20, 2000.

Pruvost, Rev. S. *The Wonders of Massabielle at Lourdes.* Translated by Rev. Joseph A. Fredette. Boston: The Lourdes Company, 1925.

Quanta Cura. Encyclical by Pope Pius IX, December 8, 1864. Accompanied by the *Syllabus of Errors.* Reproduced by The Remnant Press, n.d.

Qui Pluribus. Encyclical by Pope Pius IX, November 9, 1846. Kansas City, Mo.: Angelus Press, 1998.

Roth, Cecil. *A History of the Jews: From Earliest Times Through the Six Day War.* Revised ed. New York: Schocken Books, 1970.

Ryan, Father Abram J. *Poems: Patriotic, Religious, Miscellaneous.* New York: P. J. Kenedy & Sons, 1896.

Sarti, Roland. *Mazzini: A Life for the Religion of Politics.* Westport, Conn.: Greenwood Publishing Group, 1997.

Sharkey, Don. *The Woman Shall Conquer: The Story of the Blessed Virgin in the Modern World.* Milwaukee: Bruce Publishing Company, 1952.

Shea, John Gilmary, LL.D. *The Life of Pope Pius IX.* New York: Thomas Kelly, 1877.

Slaves of the Immaculate Heart of Mary. *Mary's Miraculous Medal.* Still River, Mass.: Slaves of the Immaculate Heart of Mary, 1999.

Smith, Denis Mack. *Italy: A Modern History*. Revised ed. Ann Arbor: University of Michigan Press, 1969.

——. *Cavour*. New York: Alfred A. Knopf, 1985.

——. *Mazzini*. New Haven, Conn.: Yale University Press, 1994.

Thompson, Edward Healy, M. A. *The Life of the Venerable Anna Maria Taigi, The Roman Matron*. New York and Cincinnati: Pustet & Co., 1883.

Thornton, Frances. *Cross Upon Cross*. New York: Benziger Brothers, 1955.

Trollope, T. Adolphus. *The Story of the Life of Pius the Ninth*. London: Richard Bentley and Son, 1877.

Ullathorne, William Bernard. *The Holy Mountain of La Salette*. London: Burns and Lambert, 1854. *Note: Publication information completed based on standard edition; confirm edition in use.*

Webster, Nesta H. *Secret Societies and Subversive Movements*. London: Boswell Publishing Company, n.d.

Woodward, Kenneth L. *Making Saints: How the Catholic Church Determines Who Becomes a Saint, Who Doesn't, and Why*. New York: Touchstone Books, 1996.

ONLINE EDITIONS AND SOURCES

Catholic Culture. "Library." https://www.catholicculture.org/culture/library/view.

Catholic Textbook Project. "Pope Pius IX Escapes from the Quirinal, November 24, 1848." https://www.catholictextbookproject.com/post/pope-pius-ix-escapes-from-the-quirinal-november-24-1848.

CRC — The League for Catholic Counter Reformation. "Founding of the League of the Catholic Counter Reformation." https://crc-internet.org/our-doctrine/catholic-counter-reformation/for-the-church/3-founding-league-crc.html.

Jewish Virtual Library. "Pope Benedict XIV on Jews." https://www.jewishvirtuallibrary.org/pope-benedict-xiv-on-jews.

Encyclopaedia Britannica. "Papal States." https://www.britannica.com/place/Papal-States.

Zadok Romanus. "The Miracle of Bl. Pius IX at St. Agnes." *Zadok Romanus* (blog), January 2008. https://zadokromanus.blogspot.com/2008/01/miracle-of-bl-piux-ix-at-st-agnes.html.

Ebert, Roger. "*Kidnapped* Film Review (2024)." *RogerEbert.com*. https://www.rogerebert.com/reviews/kidnapped-film-review-2024.

Zouave Museum. "Zouave Historical Archive." https://zouavenmuseum.nl/wp-content/uploads/2016/10/.

Papal Encyclicals Online. "The Council of Trent." https://www.papalencyclicals.net/councils/ecum20.htm.

YouTube. "Interview with Father Paul Schofield." Filmed [n.d.]. *YouTube video*, 25:42. https://www.youtube.com/watch?v=Qi9GRsHmnlI.

Papal Encyclicals Online. "Ubi Primum." Pope Pius IX. https://www.papalencyclicals.net/Pius09/p9ubipr2.htm.

ABOUT THE AUTHOR

Mark Fellows has a vocational background in law, psychology, and social work. Converting to Catholicism in 1993 changed the focus and trajectory of his life. While working professionally and raising a family of seven children, Mark was fortunate enough to find publishers for his articles and books on the Catholic faith and related subjects.

Mark has been published in the Catholic and secular press for decades. His books include *The Ninth Pius*, *A Second Coming (the Holy Shroud)*, *Fatima In Twilight*, a biography of Fatima visionary Lúcia dos Santos, a profile on J. R. R. Tolkien, and other books which can be found at https://markfellowsauthor.com/

www.ingramcontent.com/pod-product-compliance
Lightning Source LLC
Chambersburg PA
CBHW021627120626
46545CB00002B/434